Vue on Rails

End-to-End Guide to Building Web Apps Using Vue.js and Rails

Bryan Lim
Richard LaFranchi

Apress®

Vue on Rails

Bryan Lim
Singapore, Singapore

Richard LaFranchi
Boulder, CO, USA

ISBN-13 (pbk): 978-1-4842-5115-7
https://doi.org/10.1007/978-1-4842-5116-4

ISBN-13 (electronic): 978-1-4842-5116-4

Managing Director, Apress Media LLC: Welmoed Spahr
Acquisitions Editor: Louise Corrigan
Development Editor: Chris Nelson
Coordinating Editor: Nancy Chen

Cover designed by eStudioCalamar

Cover image designed by Freepik (www.freepik.com)

Distributed to the book trade worldwide by Springer Science+Business Media New York, 233 Spring Street, 6th Floor, New York, NY 10013. Phone 1-800-SPRINGER, fax (201) 348-4505, e-mail orders-ny@springer-sbm.com, or visit www.springeronline.com. Apress Media, LLC is a California LLC and the sole member (owner) is Springer Science + Business Media Finance Inc (SSBM Finance Inc). SSBM Finance Inc is a **Delaware** corporation.

For information on translations, please e-mail rights@apress.com, or visit http://www.apress.com/rights-permissions.

Apress titles may be purchased in bulk for academic, corporate, or promotional use. eBook versions and licenses are also available for most titles. For more information, reference our Print and eBook Bulk Sales web page at http://www.apress.com/bulk-sales.

Any source code or other supplementary material referenced by the author in this book is available to readers on GitHub via the book's product page, located at www.apress.com/9781484251157. For more detailed information, please visit http://www.apress.com/source-code.

Printed on acid-free paper

To Chloé, future engineer.

—Richard

Table of Contents

About the Authors..xi

About the Technical Reviewer xiii

Acknowledgments xv

Part I: Start Your Engines – The Technology 1

Chapter 1: Introduction...3

  Getting Started 3

    Hello Vue..4

    Hello Vue on Rails 5

  Our Motivation from the Beginning 6

    Who Should Read This Book?...7

    Objectives of This Book 7

    When the Price Is Right 8

  Resources: Framework Versions, Downloads, Tutorials, and More 9

    Tool Versions and Source Code 9

    Cheatsheets...10

    Useful Resources for Vue on Rails Projects.........................10

    Tools for Visual Studio 11

    Tools for VS Code..12

    Tools for Atom Editor and Sublime Text...............................13

    Who to Follow?..13

Getting Your Priorities Right: Vue First vs. Rails First 14

    Healthy Tradeoff – The Right Price 16

    Failing the Single-Page Application Litmus Test.....................................17

    KPI – Keeping Programmer Insanely Happy 17

Wrap-up and the Next Step...18

Chapter 2: Nuts and Bolts of Vue on Rails 19

Attributes of a Modern Web App 19

    What Are the Attributes of a Modern Web App?.....................................20

    Inherent Nature of Vue.js 20

    The Goodness Test..21

Asset Management 22

    Tools 22

    Should You Remove Your Old Pipe? 23

    Getting Started with Webpacker 24

Scaffolding Vue on Rails Projects 25

Rails First Approach: Putting Ruby on Rails before Vue 27

    The Yes/No Answering Robot – Version 1 27

    Evaluating the Rails-Only Approach 29

Vue First Approach: Putting Vue before Ruby on Rails 30

    The Yes/No Answering Robot – Version 2 30

    Evaluating the Vue-First Approach 33

A Good Balance: Vue as a First-Class Citizen of Rails...............................34

    The Yes/No Answering Robot – Version 3 35

    Creating Version 3 36

    Evaluating the Vue as a First-Class Citizen of Rails Approach....................37

    Reusability: A Powerful Proposition of the Vue Component.........................38

    Reactivity: Data-Binding and Virtual DOM of Vue....................................39

Wrap-up and the Next Step...39

Chapter 3: Model, Vue, and Controller 41

The Vue Instance and Other Vue Properties 41

    The Vue Lifecycle 42

el – The Main Selector of a Vue Instance 44

Props vs. Data 45

Data 46

Directives 47

@click – The Method Invoker 48

Computed Properties, Watchers, and Methods 48

Class and Style Binding 50

Plugins 51

Mixins 52

Building Vue Components 53

    Generating Vue Components for Your Vue on Rails Project 53

    Using x-template to Load Your Vue Component 54

    Communication Between Vue Components in a Rails Project 56

    Registering Components 60

Passing Data from Vue to Server 60

    With HTTP Client 62

Routing with Vue Router within a Rails Project 64

    Creating the Router File 65

    Initializing vue-router 66

    Using <router-link> 67

    Routing Parameters 68

    Redirect or Alert 69

    Points to Ponder 71

Managing State of a Rails View Using Vuex 71

    Introduction 72

    The Trouble with Vuex and Other State Management Tools..........................72

    Why Should We Manage States?...72

    Getting Started with Vuex...73

    Vuex Rails Plugin 74

  Passing Data from Server to Vue 76

    Using Action Cable as a push technology..77

    A Simple Polling 78

  Wrap-up and the Next Step...79

Part II: Hands on the Wheels – Tutorials....................................81

Chapter 4: Real-World Applications Through Short Tutorials.............83

  Specific-Page Vue Inside Rails Products...84

    Specific-Page Vue...86

    Specific-Page Vue with Turbolinks 89

  Nested Form with form-for Component..90

  Application Template of Vue on Rails Products 94

    The Template 94

    Options of Vue on Rails Application Template...95

  Vue UI Compatibility in Rails Products 97

  Manual Enabling of Vue UI in Rails Products...99

  Server-Side Rendering of Vue Components in Rails Products 100

    Scaffolding SSR Components in Rails Products 101

    Manual Configuration of SSR Vue Components in Rails Products..............103

    Internationalization...105

    Using Vue on Rails 118n 107

Simple State Management of Vue Components Inside Rails Products 110

Simple State Example 111

Scaffolding Simple State Management in Vue on Rails............................112

Wrap-up and the Next Step...113

Chapter 5: Making a Real-Time Two-Player Game with Action Cable..115

The Domain..117

The GameChannel...118

The Controllers..119

Listing Games 121

Creating a Game 122

Game Time 123

Joining a Game 125

Drawing the Tic Tac Toe Board 125

Placing a Piece..130

Accessing Action Cable from Vue..131

Wrap-up and the Next Step...132

Chapter 6: Building an Image-Cropping Tool with Vue and Active Storage 135

The Avatar 136

The User Profile...137

Vue Cropper Component 139

Loading the Image 144

Panning the Image 146

Scaling the Image 147

ImageMagick Processing...149

Wrap-up and the Next Step...151

Part III: Turbo Charge – Production Ready 153

Chapter 7: Testing, Deployment, and Troubleshooting.....................155

Testing Approaches..155

TDD – To Drive or Not to Drive? 156

What about RSpec and BDD? 157

General Testing Guidelines 157

System Tests 158

Vue Test Utilities and Jest..160

Heroku – The Ninja Deployment...165

Heroku vs. Virtual Private Server...166

Continuous Integration and Deployment 167

Troubleshooting Common Issues of Vue on Rails.............................173

Wrap-up and the Final Step 182

Chapter 8: Conclusion – Finishing the Race 183

Vue is Not Without Guilt...184

Ruby on Rails Isn't the Top in Class Either 185

Where Do You Go from Here? 185

Appendix A: The MIT License (MIT) for vuejs.org Content Used in This Book 187

Index...189

About the Authors

Bryan Lim is a web developer and contributor to open source projects like Webpacker and Vue on Rails project. He has a bachelor's degree in computing and a master's degree in business analytics from National University of Singapore. He also runs a Singapore-based software consultancy firm called Tada. You may find his Vue components, Rubygems and other open-source work on his personal website (ytbryan.com) and his Github (@ytbryan).

Richard LaFranchi is a Senior Software Engineer at Charter Communications and works on internal testing tools for the organization. He has a bachelor's degree in civil engineering from the University of Colorado, Boulder, and is currently pursuing a master's in computer science at Colorado State University. He first developed a passion for web development in 2011, and he publishes many Vue/Rails open source tutorials and projects on his GitHub (@rlafranchi).

About the Technical Reviewer

Matt is a Senior Software Engineer from Germany, interested in thoughtful software concepts with a sense of joy and elegance and a beautiful design under the hood. In the last decade of his professional career, he saw many questionable solutions inside enterprises. Vue.js and Rails are different frameworks with the special power of supportive and helpful communities behind. You can follow him on his Github or Twitter (@m5o).

Acknowledgments

The authors would like to recognize all developers and engineers who have committed their time to supporting open source software. The list is vast, but the most notable in the Vue and Rails communities are listed here:

- Evan You – Vue creator

- Yukihiro Matsumoto – Ruby creator

- David Heinemeier Hansson (DHH) – Ruby on Rails creator

- Aaron Patterson – Ruby on Rails core team

- Sarah Drasner – Vue core team

- Chris Fritz – Vue core team

PART I

Start Your Engines – The Technology

Chapter 1. Introduction

Chapter 2. Nuts and Bolts of Vue on Rails

Chapter 3. Model, Vue, and Controller

Start Your Engines — The Technology

CHAPTER 1

Introduction

How do you know so much about computer? I did not, it was the first one.

—Grace Hopper

This chapter is an introduction to the world of Vue and Rails – two open source web frameworks that focus on developer happiness. In this chapter, we will take a closer look at why we write this book, some of the priorities when developing Vue on Rails project, and what are the available tools for Vue on Rails development.

Getting Started

Ruby on Rails developers tend to have a love–hate relationship with JavaScript, but the community is beginning to embrace JavaScript. In 2014, a JavaScript framework Vue.js was created. Vue's entry into the development world changes how we do frontend, just like how Rails changed web development in 2004. This book contains our research on how to make this marriage of Vue and Rails work to stand the test of time.

So, the question arises, how do I integrate frontend technologies with Ruby on Rails? Do I build a single-page application or do I use JavaScript only when necessary? Why should a web developer use Vue.js or Ruby on Rails? (Chapter 2) If I am using Vue.js, how do I scaffold a Vue component in Ruby on Rails? (Chapter 2) How do I configure my Vue.js in a Ruby on

© Bryan Lim and Richard LaFranchi 2019
B. Lim and R. LaFranchi, *Vue on Rails*, https://doi.org/10.1007/978-1-4842-5116-4_1

Rails project? How do I save time and doing these with the least amount of time? (Chapter 4)

We will take a closer look at each question in the subsequent topics and chapters.

Hello Vue

It has never been a better time to be a web developer.

The Web is getting faster than ever. HTTP/2 is coming which means data can be transmitted on the Web a whole lot faster. Faster and better build tools like parcel.js push the limit for configuration-less and fast bundling of web assets. Parcel.js announced its support for Vue.js recently. Faster applications and web servers like NGINX Unit may get integrated to Ruby on Rails soon. The Web is also getting decentralized with peer-browsing technology and peer-to-peer protocol. One such P2P browser is the beaker browser project. Firefox has also included the decentralizing peer-to-peer protocol in its latest release.

Being a web developer means that we have more control over the destiny of our software application as a craftsman or as a small development team.

Just like how Rails revolutionized web development in 2004, Vue.js is the new kid on the block that changes the way we design and code modern UIs on the Web. Vue shows us that it does not need to be convoluted or introduce a new templating design over HTML to make web page reactive.

The following code example presents a simple two-way binding through a data variable "message":

```
<div id="app">
  {{ message }}
</div>

var app = new Vue ({
  el: '#app',
```

```
  data: {
    message: 'Hello Vue!'
  }
})
```

Plain and simple at its beautiful core.

The straightforward syntax of Vue gives rise to a form of clarity that is needed in today's convoluted JavaScript environment. This JavaScript convolution refers to the complication added via JavaScript into the HTML and CSS layers. As web app grows, this complication increases. And Vue.js fixes this convolution through the encapsulation of each JavaScript responsibility in the form of Vue component and its component architecture. Each component holds a single responsibility, and this will be further demonstrated in Chapter 2. Furthermore, you will be delighted to find such obvious syntax sprinkled throughout the Vue.js framework, making web programming fun and easy.

And if the Vue core library is not impressive enough, Vue, like Ruby on Rails, puts good communication as its top priority. Vue.js just announced the launch of the cookbook for Vue.js which emphasizes in-depth and focused examples of each aspect of Vue.js. Vue.js also comes with a great community, clear documentation, dynamic tools, and library ecosystem, some of which we outline later in this chapter. All batteries are included.

Now, it's up to the web developers to figure out how to make these two great frameworks work together.

Hello Vue on Rails

But it takes two to tango or two hands to clap. A Vue on Rails integration is only possible with the blessings from both frameworks. Fortunately, both frameworks are built in ways that lend themselves to such integration.

For its part, Ruby on Rails has a big tent philosophy by welcoming other frameworks to integrate with it via project Webpacker.

On the other hand, Vue.js is both backend agnostic and progressive in its kernel. This means that a developer can choose to integrate part of its features without adopting wholesale. This makes Vue.js extremely powerful and versatile.

Vue on Rails is a modern web architecture that ships meaning default configuration and component generator to ease component creation. It embraces Turbolinks and treats Vue as a first-class entity. Each component within such architecture has its own component tests and features. Vue on Rails represents a movement where the future of web application development is hopeful without the complexity of a convoluted architecture.

Our Motivation from the Beginning

Around early 2016, I was trying out Vue.js in some of my side projects and research on how to integrate it effectively into my Ruby on Rails projects. I find Vue to be approachable, and because of its progressive nature, it is a versatile framework to work with.

At the same time in 2016, Richard started writing tutorials on Vue. js and Ruby on Rails on his blog. And later on, he announced his plan of writing a book on Vue.js and Ruby on Rails. I thought to myself that it will be a good opportunity to reach out to him in case he needs a co-author. To my surprise, Richard was planning to message me.

This *Vue on Rails* book is written because of our love for web programming and web applications.

Vue.js with Ruby on Rails is complimentary and lightweight and forms the current best tools to build the next version of your modern web application. Vue.js can be easily added to legacy Rails projects that want to modernize their application. And it can be done without an entire rewrite of the application.

This book encompasses the next stage of our research on Vue.js and Ruby on Rails so that others may benefit from the union of these two great frameworks, its tools and library ecosystem and its community.

Vue on Rails book also represents the value of freedom. The freedom that two authors from two different parts of the world can be writing on two open source technologies that will change the way we make things on the Internet moving forward.

Vue on Rails will liberalize the way you make your web application in a sustainable way.

Who Should Read This Book?

This book is written for the ordinary web developer concerning about the best web technology to build a modern web application, doing all these without compromising on their happiness at work.

Vue on Rails book also is written for project managers and technical leads evaluating the next tools to add to your arsenal of technologies in their workplace.

For existing Rails developers who are looking for an approachable Javascript framework that are progressive and fit into your technology stack and team.

For existing Vue developers who are looking beyond the Node community, Ruby on Rails opens you a new world of Ruby and Rails community.

Objectives of This Book

Vue on Rails approach offers a complete end-to-end solution to create modern web applications with a modern UI flow.

This book aims to save you hundreds of hours learning how to integrate Vue.js and Ruby on Rails, with meaning default configuration and useful generators to scaffold your component parts, Jest tests, Vue-UI compatibility, and more.

Furthermore, this book will focus on some concepts like Rails-first Vue-first class approach and specific-page vue technique vs. single-page application and demonstrates various integrations of Vue.js with Ruby on Rails's technology like Action Cable or Rails' API.

Vue on Rails book aims to cover both the beginner topics of Vue on Rails while dropping wisdom that may delight intermediate or advanced folks on web app development. This book emphasizes on component-based architecture which we think is the next frontier for modern web user interface.

This book is guided by the following principles:

- Choosing convention over configuration

- Optimizing for programmer's happiness

- Picking simple over complex (when the price is right)

You may notice two of the principles coming from Ruby on Rails' doctrine (`https://rubyonrails.org/doctrine/`), while the last one is inspired by Occam's razor. The Rails doctrine is a set of nine principles that set the direction and foundation of Ruby on Rails as a web development framework. This book took a leaf from the doctrine Finally, we hope that this book to be more illuminating than informative to you on your Vue on Rails learning journey.

Recommendation   To read more about the Ruby on Rails doctrine `https://rubyonrails.org/doctrine/` and Occam's razor `www.math.ucr.edu/home/baez/physics/General/occam.html`

When the Price Is Right

The price of developing an application gets expensive overtime due to the overcrowding impact of your convoluted code. Developer productivity decreased and the time taken to add new feature or fix existing bug increases. There may also be too many components residing inside your

Rails project. As the developers allow certain parts of their Rails project to grow and increase in importance, the price of that component will also increase. Therefore, we need a better way to arrange existing components as well as maintaining the total cost and health of your entire project. These will be covered in Chapter 2 and Chapter 7 through testing.

In Vue on Rails, we call such important component a first-class component. Somewhat like a first-class citizen ought to be in his/her own country.

Resources: Framework Versions, Downloads, Tutorials, and More

This book comes with free hands-on code and cheatsheets that you may be interested to use for the next Vue on Rails project. This section identifies the key tools, cheatsheets, and where you can find them. Both Vue and Rails are great frameworks with good documentation, great community, awesome tutorial, and webcast that set them apart from other web frameworks. This section also references some of the particularly useful resources.

Tool Versions and Source Code

This book will contain code examples and tutorial that uses the following version of each tool:

- Ruby 2.5.3 `https://github.com/ruby/ruby`

- Rails 5.2.1 `https://github.com/rails/rails`

- Webpacker 3.5 `https://github.com/rails/webpacker`

- Node.js `https://github.com/nodejs/node`

- Babel `https://github.com/babel/babel`

- Vue 2.5.16 `https://github.com/vuejs/vue`

- Webpack 4 `www.github.com/webpack/webpack`

- Yarn 1.2.1 `https://github.com/yarnpkg/yarn`

- Vue on Rails `http://github.com/vueonrails/vueonrails`

We are also using VS Code for writing code.

To download the hands-on code:

- `https://github.com/vueonrails/code-examples`

Cheatsheets

Get up to speed with each framework with the help of cheatsheets:

- Vue.js cheatsheet `https://www.vuemastery.com/vue-cheat-sheet`

- Ruby on Rails cheatsheet `http://staff.um.edu.mt/alexiei.dingli/IntroductionToWS/Lectures/ruby-on-rails-cheat-sheet-v1.pdf`

- Vue on Rails cheatsheet `http://github.com/vueonrails/cheatsheet`

Useful Resources for Vue on Rails Projects

The following resources all are well worth referencing:

- Official Vue.js guide – The official Vue.js documentation to jumpstart your frontend development using Vue.js `https://vuejs.org/v2/guide/`

- Official Vue.js cookbook – The cookbook provides examples for common and interesting use cases `https://vuejs.org/v2/cookbook`

- Official Rails guide – The official Ruby on Rails documentation to jumpstart your web development using the favorite ruby web framework `http://guides.rubyonrails.org`

- A list of awesome Vue resources – A GitHub repository about Vue.js resources `https://github.com/vuejs/awesome-vue`

- Stackoverflow questions on Vue and Rails `https://stackoverflow.com/questions/tagged/vue.js+ruby-on-rails`

- Vue components – Repositories of components `https://vuecomponents.com`

- Official Vue-curated components – A list of curated components from Vue `https://curated.vuejs.org`

- Vue toolbox – Another curated list of components `http://www.vuetoolbox.com`

- A GitHub search for Vue things `https://github.com/search?o=desc&q=vue&s=stars&type=Repositories`

Tools for Visual Studio

Visual Studio is a development editor and environment from Microsoft. It is the precursor of Visual Studio Code and it is written in the following:

- Vue.js pack 2017 – A Visual Studio extension that contains HTML intellisense and code snippets for the Vue.js JavaScript Library `https://marketplace.visualstudio.com/items?itemName=MadsKristensen.VuejsPack-18329`

Tools for VS Code

VS Code is a code editor made by Microsoft. It is the most popular code editor with a customized theme and plugins platform.

Read more at `https://code.visualstudio.com`. To download VS Code, `https://code.visualstudio.com/Download`

- <Insert Our Vue on Rails extensions> `https://github.com/vueonrails/vueonrails-extensionpack`

- Sarah's Vue.js extensions – A collection of extension for working with Vue development in VS Code editor `https://marketplace.visualstudio.com/items?itemName=sdras.vue-vscode-extensionpack`

- Vetur – Vue tooling for VS Code editor. It includes syntax highlighting, snippet, autocompletion, error checking, and more. This is a must-have extension `https://marketplace.visualstudio.com/items?itemName=octref.vetur`

- Vue 2 Snippets – A popular VS Code extension that include Vue2 code snippet `https://marketplace.visualstudio.com/items?itemName=hollowtree.vue-snippets`

- Vue VS Code snippet – A VS Code extension that helps you to write less with code snippet `https://marketplace.visualstudio.com/items?itemName=sdras.vue-vscode-snippets`

Tools for Atom Editor and Sublime Text

Atom Editor is a code editor made by GitHub. Read more at `https://atom.io`. Sublime Text is another popular code editor that is similar with Atom Editor but was created much earlier. Read more at `http://sublimetext.com/`

- Vue Format `https://atom.io/packages/vue-format`

- Language Vue `https://atom.io/packages/language-vue`

- Vue Syntax Highlight `https://github.com/vuejs/vue-syntax-highlight`

Who to Follow?

A list of people to follow for continuous learning of Vue on Rails beyond this book

Ruby on Rails

- David Heinemeier Hansen – The creator of Ruby on Rails `https://github.com/dhh`

- Gaurav Tiwari – The maintainer of Webpacker project `https://github.com/gauravtiwari`

- Javan Makhmali – A Rails veteran, contributor of webpacker project and the creator of various popular repo like trix, stimulusjs, whenever rubygem `https://github.com/javan`

- The full list of Rails core team and alumni `https://github.com/orgs/rails/people`

Vue.js

- Evan You – The creator of Vue.js `http://github.com/yyx990803`

- Edd Yerburgh – A Vue core team member and expert in Vue testing `https://github.com/eddyerburgh`

- Chris Fritz – A Vue core team member and a Vue veteran `https://github.com/chrisvfritz`

- Guilaume Chau – A Vue core team member `https://github.com/akryum`

- Pine – A Vue core team member and creator of vetur `https://github.com/octref`

- The full list of Vue.js core team and alumni `https://github.com/orgs/vuejs/people`

For further questions, you may also reach out to the authors:

- Richard LaFranchi `https://github.com/rlafranchi`

- Bryan Lim `http://github.com/ytbryan`

Getting Your Priorities Right: Vue First vs. Rails First

This section focuses on the priorities of Vue on Rails projects. To get the web application development right, we need to get its priorities right first because all priorities lead to a certain development outcome. This is especially true when there are two great frameworks residing in a single web project structure. This section will explore some questions that will set you on the correct path while you get started in making your Vue on Rails app.

The right priorities for your web application:

- Maintainability of the web application project

- Efficient of the web application

- Security of the web application

- Within team budget of the web application development

- Maximizing programmer happiness

- Minimal complexity of the code base

- Design architecture extensibility of the web application

- User interface and usability of the web application

And this list can go on endlessly as you expand on each expectation.

But what are the important priorities? Which architecture will support the most priorities in the web application moving forward? Identifying the "right" priorities does not mean balancing all of them. It is to deliberately choose a healthy number of these targets while maximizing a programmer's happiness.

Every project has different requirements and features. But there is a common feature and requirement found in all project that forms part of the priorities. Every project differs from the others, but one thing stands out in common: the need to have users for the web application.

Some reasonable Vue on Rails questions you may have in mind include:

- How do you structure your Vue on Rails project?

- How do you test your Vue code?

- How do you use the best features of Vue inside Ruby on Rails project?

- How do you have the best security on my Vue on Rails projects?

- How do you have an extensible architecture that is not over complex?

- How can you achieve a modern UI?

- How do you achieve all these without making too big a tradeoff?

- Regarding tradeoff, what is the right price?

Healthy Tradeoff – The Right Price

Tradeoffs are common during development of a software. If you can make a set of healthy tradeoffs, you are on the right path to successful completion of your web application. In the case of Vue on Rails, two crossroads are met, and we must decide. They are namely the Vue on Rails' project structure and the choice of router, that is, whether to use Vue routing or Rails routing.

A project structure is the way files and folders are organized in a project repository. There is a fine balance between project structure and organization, and sometimes tradeoffs are required to get the right balance of following a structure and keeping things simple. Model View, Controller architecture has stood the test of time. We think that JavaScript sprinkles are just components. The risk is that calling it component will make it so big that they might be too big to become a liability. But a wheel is never the main component of a car. But the car cannot move forward if one of the wheels broke down. Therefore, there is a natural constraint to prevent any component to become too big and become the product itself.

Single-page application has no such constraints on project structure, so you often find thousands of boilerplate examples of JavaScript projects that don't follow any conventions or standards.

Failing the Single-Page Application Litmus Test

Single-page application (SPA) is an architecture choice where the code is divided into frontend user interface and a backend API. SPA gets its name by having a single-page load at the start with subsequent user interaction causing further addition in resources onto the web page. SPA requires a bigger development team with at least two groups of developers: frontend and backend right from the start.

SPA is commonly compared with the monolithic architecture that Rails is famous for. A monolithic architecture is an architecture where all services live in a single code base. Many organizations have adopted a service-oriented architecture in recent years, but we believe that this may be a mistake for small businesses and development teams. Vue on Rails purposefully chose to continue the monolithic path because of its ease of usage for the developers. It is more sustainable for smaller development team without big enterprise budget.

KPI – Keeping Programmer Insanely Happy

We cannot do all these without a backend as great as Rails with a Rails core team that is dedicated to developer happiness. We also cannot do this without a frontend that is focus on the similar pursuit of happiness without overly dominating in the way you control your user interface. The Vue on Rails approach follows the happy list, which also applies to our daily lives outside of programming.

- Tons of family time

- Remote work

- Enough sleep

- Manageable and maintainable web app

- Insane amount of programmer happiness

Flip each item on the happy list and you will get Keep Programmer Insane. We oppose the 80-hour work week that many in the startup culture have adopted, because we believe it is counterproductive and just causes developer burnout and ultimate failure of a project.

Wrap-up and the Next Step

With two great web frameworks in one, Vue on Rails is standing firm in this modern world of web development. Programmers can benefit from tools and shortcuts from both Vue and Rails world to tackle their endless pursuit of development in this capitalist world.

For a Vue on Rails project, what should be the right architecture? Should we adopt a Vue-first or Rails-first approach? The answer to this question forms the premise and the overall approach of this book. We will be examining and taking a closer look at several topics like asset management in the new Ruby on Rails and single-page application vs. monolithics architecture and evaluate thedifferent approaches to integrate Vue into Rails. These topics set the foundation of discussion for later chapters of this book.

CHAPTER 2

Nuts and Bolts of Vue on Rails

A user interface should be so simple that a beginner in an emergency can understand it within ten seconds.

—Ted Nelson

This chapter covers the attributes of a modern web application, the nature of Vue.js, choices in managing assets on Ruby on Rails, and the approaches towards integrating Vue into Ruby on Rails project. We will walk through a few examples of how to approach a Vue integration with Ruby on Rails and compare this to the traditional Ruby on Rails approach.

Attributes of a Modern Web App

A web application is one that uses web technologies, namely, HTML, CSS, and JavaScript, as the building blocks of a final software product. A web app requires some form of web-rendering technology like an Internet browser, a WebView, or any future rendering technology to display its final product.

Web apps offer the benefits of cross-platform development where a small code base can be reused across different software platforms like MacOS, Window, Linux, mobile iOS, and Android. This translates into cost saving in development budget and developer productivity at its best.

© Bryan Lim and Richard LaFranchi 2019
B. Lim and R. LaFranchi, *Vue on Rails*, https://doi.org/10.1007/978-1-4842-5116-4_2

Further, some native iPhone and Android apps use a web app to form part of its entire technology stack. A mixture of web and native features within an app is called a *hybrid* app.

A modern web app is simply one that is using the latest–greatest web technology and is up to date with most web standards and best practices.

What Are the Attributes of a Modern Web App?

The mainstream understanding of a modern web application includes the following attributes, which we can back up by highlighting some attributes that Vue.js naturally inherits.

- Cross platform

- Compliance with major web browsers and web protocol

- Simple and concise code base

- Clean and loosely coupled architecture

- Ease of testing

- Flexible configurationModern UI flow that is responsive and fluid

- Fast loading

- Intuitive

Inherent Nature of Vue.js

Vue.js naturally fulfills the preceding attributes, and we can highlight some of the reasons why it is a great library to use in the modern Web.

1. Vue is highly compatible with modern web browsers. This also means it works across platforms and compliant with major web protocol.

2. Vue is fast and small in size.

3. Since Vue is only a library for building a user interface and is highly progressive, it can integrate well with any other full-web framework without creating a complex code base or architecture.

4. Vue ships with testing utilities.

5. Vue allows dynamic and responsive design.

6. Vue has the following: reactive system, data binding, virtual-DOM management, state management, and more.

7. Vue allows a component-based architecture to be integrated with any framework.

8. Vue code is intuitive to developers, so naturally it helps with building an intuitive user experience.

The Goodness Test

In the world of web technology, the contemporary is temporary. The modern becomes old in a year time. What we find lacking in a modern web application are similar attributes that we find in the modest and old antique furniture or old wine. The older the better. A lack of modesty in a user interface is also an unfortunate part of a modern web application where every web app aims to be overly responsive in nature. Are the preceding attributes truly a set of good gauge to define a good modern web application? Is it consistently good? Does it feel good? Is there evidence from the structure that it is good?

What makes a modern web application good is its ability to solve today's real-world problems in a manner that is intuitive as possible to its users. On top of intuition, web applications must behave as expected, so actions produce the expected results, and it must perform quickly. In reality, the users of an application determine the Goodness Test, but as developers we want to deliver that in a way that is simple, so the tools that allow us to do this determine the Goodness Test from a developer's perspective. Bringing in a library such as Vue into the Ruby on Rails world opens up an opportunity to revisit the tools we use for asset management that is how to manage static content such as images, CSS, fonts, and JavaScript.

Asset Management

Asset management is how we manage static files such as images, CSS, Javascript, and font files in a web application. For traditional MVC frameworks, the tools used for asset management plays an important role to faciliate the development of a modern web application. In this section, we look at some of these tools and their roles in Ruby on Rails.

Tools

Ruby on Rails uses the asset pipeline and sprockets to manage assets; we will discuss this along with Webpack and the integration of Webpack into Ruby on Rails using the Webpacker gem.

Asset Pipeline

The asset pipeline is an internal framework of Ruby on Rails to manage Javascript, stylesheets, images, and other assets. It is powered by the `sprockets-rails` gem. The purpose of the asset pipeline is to streamline the build process for static assets using one simple command.

```
rake assets:precompile
```

The asset pipeline has traditionally used sprockets which is a tool for compiling scss/sass files into CSS, managing the digest hashes for assets for cache busting, and using minifying/uglifying assets along with some compression techniques such as gzip.

It allows assets in your application to be automatically combined with assets from other gems. For example, jQuery-rails includes a copy of jquery.js and enables AJAX features in Rails views.

Webpack

Webpack is a module bundler for the Web that is deemed to be the future for web framework using JavaScript. Rails started a project called Webpacker, a thin wrapper around webpack together with a JavaScript package installer called Yarn, to help programmers build JavaScript app on Ruby on Rails.

Webpacker

Webpacker is a wrapper around webpack and yarn. It makes it easy to use the JavaScript pre-processor and bundler ability of webpack to manage application-like JavaScript in Rails.

It co-exists with the asset pipeline, as the primary purpose for webpack is app-like JavaScript, not images, CSS, or even JavaScript Sprinkles (that all continues to live in app/assets). However, it is possible to use Webpacker for CSS, images, and fonts assets as well, in which case you may not even need the asset pipeline. This is mostly relevant when exclusively using component-based JavaScript frameworks.

Should You Remove Your Old Pipe?

Since Webpacker is created to co-exist with your sprockets asset pipeline. The answer is not yet; there is no need to remove the asset pipeline especially for legacy applications that you want to start integrating Vue into. There may be a point where Ruby on Rails abandons sprockets, so it might be required to migrate assets to Webpacker in future versions. For new applications, we recommend starting with Webpacker for asset management.

Our advice is not to move towards Webpacker for your entire assets immediately, but allow Webpacker to manage the assets of your component while leaving the rest of your assets to assets pipeline. Webpacker is a major shift in how to manage assets, since legacy Rails applications use a lot of gems that assume use of the asset pipeline and sprockets, whereas Webpacker uses yarn where packages are retrieved from npmjs.org. So it is important to consider the nature of your application and how to proceed with asset management. We'll discuss how to use Webpacker using tools we have develop to make Vue integration seamless.

Getting Started with Webpacker

Webpacker is a wrapper around webpack and yarn. It makes it easy to use the JavaScript pre-processor and bundler ability of webpack to manage application-like JavaScript in Rails.

It co-exists with the asset pipeline, as the primary purpose for webpack is app-like JavaScript, not images, CSS, or even JavaScript Sprinkles (that all continues to live in app/assets). However, it is possible to use Webpacker for CSS, images, and fonts assets as well, in which case you may not even need the asset pipeline. This is mostly relevant when exclusively using component-based JavaScript frameworks.

Webpacker is essential for the approach we will follow throughout this book. It allows scaffolding of new Vue component and allows embedding of the component onto Rails views. The latest Webpacker ships with webpack 4.x and latest babel. This means we will enjoy free performance upgrade of webpack including the split chunk api and other benefits. You are encouraged to use Webpacker 4 in Ruby on Rails moving forward.

Installing Webpacker

Installing Webpacker is as simple as adding it to your Gemfile and running a couple of commands.

1. #At Gemfile

    ```
    gem 'webpacker'
    ```

2. Install webpacker and its dependencies:

    ```
    bundle install
    rails webpacker:install
    ```

3. Install Vue and its basic dependencies:

    ```
    rails webpacker:install:vue
    ```

Now that you are up and running with Webpacker, we'll discuss the vueonrails gem and how to use it for Vue component scaffolding.

Scaffolding Vue on Rails Projects

Often times we need a simple and easy way to scaffold Vue component and its dependencies onto Ruby on Rails project. In this section, the vueonrails Ruby gem will be used to scaffold a Vue on Rails project with all its necessary configuration and dependencies we will need for a single component.

1. Add the vueonrails gem onto your Gemfile as well as the webpacker gem if it is not already there.

    ```
    gem 'vueonrails'
    gem 'webpacker'
    ```

2. Next, set up the project with an install generator:

```
bundle install
yarn install
rails webpacker:install
rails webpacker:install:vue
rails vue:setup
```

This runs `rails webpacker:install` and
`rails webpacker:install:vue` and adds other
dependencies like Vuex, Vue_component helpers, to
your arsenal of tools.

3. Now generate a Vue component called home:

```
rails generate vue home
```

4. Let us create a Rails view using the controller
generator:

```
rails generate controller pages home
```

5. Now, add the component pack tag along with
the stylesheet pack tag to `app/vies/layouts/`
`application.html.erb`:

```
<%= javascript_pack_tag "home" %>
<%= stylesheet_pack_tag "home" %>
```

6. You can run `http://localhost:3000/pages/home`
to see your Vue component on a Rails page after
starting the dev server:

```
rails server
```

Using the Vue component scaffold, you can have a Vue component on your Rails project the quick and easy way. If you find these steps tedious, we made an application template that will get you up to speed in a single command. The template is available at `https://vueonrails.com/vue` and the command creates a new Vue on Rails-ready application.

```
rails new app -m https://vueonrails.com/vue -d postgresql
```

Rails First Approach: Putting Ruby on Rails before Vue

Consider the following simple example of a Yes/No answering robot. In this example, we will use only Ruby on Rails and its provided jQuery to build this example.

The Yes/No Answering Robot – Version 1

Follow these steps for our version 1 example:

1. Let's create an empty Rails project:

   ```
   rails new v1_robot
   rails generate scaffold pages
   rails db:migrate
   ```

2. Next, copy and paste the following to app/views/pages/index.html.erb:

   ```erb
   <%= form_tag("/pages/search", method: "get", remote: true) do %>
     <%= label_tag(:q, "Please ask a yes or no question. For example: Is the sky blue?") %><br>
     <%= text_field_tag(:q) %>
   ```

```
  <%= submit_tag("Search") %>
<% end %>

<div id="result"></div>
```

3. Add the search action to the pages controller in app/
   controllers/pages_controller.rb

```ruby
def search
  @answer = ((rand(10)%2) == 1) ? "Yes" : "No"
end
```

4. Use JS format to respond at app/views/pages/
   search.js.erb:

```erb
$("result").text("<%= escape_javascript(@answer) %>");
```

5. Add the following JavaScript to app/assets/
   javascript/pages.js:

```javascript
$(document).ready(function() {
  $("#q").on( "input", function() {
    question()
  })
})

function question(){
  $("#result").val = 'Waiting for you to stop
  typing...'
  getAnswer()
}

function getAnswer(){
  if ($("#q").val().indexOf('?') === -1) {
    $("#result").text('Questions usually contain a
    question mark. :)')
```

```
    return
  }

  $("#result").text('Thinking...')
}
```

So we've created a new Rails app that takes in a simple form that takes a question and randomly returns an answer of Yes or No. The answer is returned without re-rendering the page using the search endpoint with a js format. We add some JavaScript to add some client side validation for ensuring the question contains a question mark and inform the user that the robot is thinking about an answer while the answer is fetched from the backend. Next, we will evaluate this approach.

Evaluating the Rails-Only Approach

The patching of functionality via jQuery works. But can JavaScript be treated as a first-class asset than some working patchwork? As the app becomes bigger, the patchwork may lead to a "JavaScript soup" where JavaScript becomes more like a liability than a liberty of the web view.

Updating virtual DOM is cheaper than DOM. While jQuery is a DOM library, this approach did not leverage on the development of the virtual DOM. There is also a lack of data binding, reactivity, and other things including state management. These issues may become obvious as the answering robot becomes more complex.

Can a Vue-first approach solve some of the problems that Ruby on Rails and jQuery is limited to? Will Vue.js displace jQuery? What are some of the features that a Vue-first approach offer? We will evaluate a Vue-first approach in the next section.

Vue First Approach: Putting Vue before Ruby on Rails

In this section, we will be using a Vue-first approach with a single-page application and a Ruby on Rails API application:

- It will be a single-page application where a web page is created so that it adds or subtracts dynamically through user interaction instead of rendering the same web page via the server. We will use vue-cli to generate the single-page application.

- We will be reusing the backend from Rails-only approach for simplicity sake.

The Yes/No Answering Robot – Version 2

Follow these steps for our version 2 example:

1. Let's install vue-cli:

   ```
   yarn install vue-cli
   ```

2. Now, let's create a project called v2_robot:

   ```
   vue create v2_robot
   ```

3. Next, create the following src/robot/robot.vue:

   ```
   <template>
     <div>
       <label>Please ask a yes or no question.
         For example: Is the sky blue? </label>
       <input v-model="question">
       <button>Search</button>
   ```

```
    <p>{{ answer }}</p>
  </div>
</template>
```

4. Create the following src/robot/robot.js. Axios is used as an HTTP client to communicate with the Ruby on Rails API backend.

```
// import _ from 'lodash'
import axios from 'axios'

export default {
data: function () {
  return {
    question: "",
    answer: ""
  }
},
watch: {
  question: function () {
    this.answer = 'Waiting for you to stop typing...'
    this.getAnswer()
  }
},
methods: {
  getAnswer: _.debounce(
    function () {
      if (this.question.indexOf('?') === -1) {
        this.answer = 'Questions usually contain a
        question mark. :)'
        return
      }
```

```
        this.answer = 'Thinking...'
        var vm = this
        axios.get('https://yesno.wtf/api')
          .then(function (response) {
            vm.answer = _.capitalize(response.data.
            answer)
          })
          .catch(function (error) {
            vm.answer = 'Error! Could not reach the
            API. ' + error
          })
      },
      500
    )
  }
}
```

27. Search endpoint in a JSON format:

```
def search
  answer = ((rand(10)%2) == 1) ? "Yes" : "No"
  render json: {answer: answer}
end
```

28. Start the vue-cli server:

```
vue serve
```

29. At a separate terminal, start your Ruby on Rails API
    server:

```
rails server
```

30. Visit http://localhost:8080 to see your Vue app.

Evaluating the Vue-First Approach

There are both favorable and unfavorable aspects to the Vue-first approach. Let's consider both the pros and the cons.

Pros:

- Having an unobtrusive reactivity by leveraging on an asynchronous virtual DOM update

- Having clear separation of client and server responsibilities. Useful for a big team with a sizable budget

- Making it desirable for teams with dedicated frontend and backend developers

- Having more room to build a complex and dedicated user interface

- Having a simple and clean syntax. Not reinventing the wheel but reusing the HTML syntax

- Allowing component-based architecture for code reusing

- Being extremely progressive in nature. Allow incremental improvement of the user interface

- Making it useful for existing applications that require or already expose an API

Cons:

- Juggling with two project directories (Vue-cli and Rails) can be a pain.

- Abandoning Ruby on Rails helpers. For instance, form helpers becoming obsolete.

- Abandoning Ruby on Rails router becomes obsolete in favor of Vue Router.

- Lacking a clear and supported interface for interacting with Ruby on Rails.

- Having a component-based structure is not always straightforward and may add complexity to the application.

This approach will generate a more dynamic answering robot since Vue.js is reactive; the web page does not require a web page refresh.

Moreover, there is an increase in supporting libraries from two ecosystems. This may be a double-edged sword as more tools do not mean getting more work done.

This approach increases the complexity by having to juggle two project structures that are bind by a loosely coupled JSON API. There is also a need to relearn routing in a Vue.js application if you are a Ruby on Rails developer.

All in all, the rabbit hole of diving into Vue.js with a single-page application making Ruby on Rails a backend only solution is too risky.

Is Vue-first with Rails API the best way to build a web application? Could there be an easier way to integrate Vue.js without going to juggling two projects structures for one web application product? Let's find out in the next section.

A Good Balance: Vue as a First-Class Citizen of Rails

We want to achieve the best of both worlds and do what works. In this section we'll use an approach that uses Webpacker and streamlines Vue integration.

The Yes/No Answering Robot – Version 3

If you are not satisfied with either the Vue-first or Rails-only approach, we share the same sentiment.

In this version of the Yes/No answer robot, we will use Rails' Webpacker to deliver a Vue-first class and Rails-first approach to building a web application. The idea is to follow Ruby on Rails conventions and the traditional MVC pattern (2-1a) and take advantage of Vue for components of the application that requires interactive elements (2-1b).

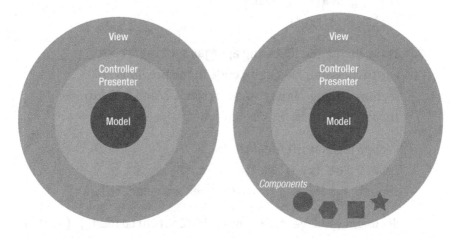

Figure 2-1. *Traditional MVC pattern (left) and MVC with components in the view layer (right)*

Vue on Rails project shouldn't be about conquering every web page with a single-page application. It should start with conquering each component and trying to reuse them on the relevant web page.

Webpacker is an efficient way to divide a web page into important components and let Vue do the heavy lifting for a more complex interface.

Webpacker also provides a clean and clear interface for Vue.js to interact with Ruby on Rails, and it ships with some basic configuration of Vue Webpacker configuration.

Creating Version 3

Let's get started in making version 3 of the Yes/No answering robot.

1. Initialize a new rails app with the Vue webpack integration.

   ```
   rails new v3_robot --webpack=vue
   ```

2. Next, at your terminal, run the following:

   ```
   rails g scaffold pages
   rails db:migrate
   ```

3. Then, create the following app/javascript/robot. vue to the same JavaScript code in the previous section. Change import App from '../app.vue' to import App from '../robot.vue':

   ```
   //app/javascript/search.js
   import Vue from 'vue'
   import App from '../robot.vue' #change this

   document.addEventListener('DOMContentLoaded', () => {
     const el = document.body.appendChild(document.
   createElement('search'))
     const app = new Vue({
       el,
       render: h => h(App)
     })
     console.log(app)
   })
   ```

4. Next, at your `app/views/pages/index.html.erb`, replace the entire page with the following code:

```
<!-- app/views/pages/index.html.erb -->
<%= javascript_pack_tag "robot" %>
```

5. At your terminal, run this

```
rails server
```

6. Please visit `http://localhost:3000/pages` to see the robot.

Evaluating the Vue as a First-Class Citizen of Rails Approach

Like other approaches, this one also has its pros and cons, though as we'll see it is more favorable overall.

Pros

- Having access to both Vue.js and Ruby on Rails ecosystem in your toolbelt

- Enjoying the clean interface of webpacker and separation of concern of frontend component and backend API

- Enjoying the best of Vue – True unobtrusive reactivity and asynchronous virtual DOM update

- Enjoying component-based architecture on top of the model view-controller framework

- Retaining the Ruby on Rails helpers for programmers' happiness

- Having a simpler architecture than a single-page application architecture

- Having the ease of upgrading and maintaining on both Vue and Rails

Cons

- Having a monolithic application may not be suitable for a big development team.

- Having a Vue component delivered through Webpacker may result in tight coupling when compared to a single-page application with total separation of frontend/backend responsibility.

- Having too many Vue components may complicate the Rails' view.

This is a completely different approach where we do not do a surgical procedure on Ruby on Rails or Vue to make them work together. Rather, through Webpacker, we deliver the best of Vue on top of the Ruby on Rails model view-controller architecture. This architecture allows us to follow traditional Rails conventions but allows us to take advantage of the simplicity of Vue and add in components when plain old JavaScript may be too bloated for what you are trying to accomplish.

The caveat is that we assume a small team of 2-4 developers for a small-to medium-sized web application. But this approach may not be desirable for a smaller team or a single programmer where resources are limited.

Reusability: A Powerful Proposition of the Vue Component

Most web pages do not need a complex UI. Not all pages will have a full-fledged calendar or text editor, to begin with. But when you need a complex interface, a component-based architecture will help.

A component-based architecture diversifies the Rails views towards modern user interface with the support of Rails API.

Each component packs all the Vue.js goodness into a manageable object. And each component is a Vue instance. It allows reusable code by extending HTML code. Furthermore, Vue component allows you to enjoy access to a Vue's lifecycle and reactive nature of Vue.js and, above all, have all these in a progressive and reusable manner.

All in all, Vue component offers a systematic way to organize complex user interface into a component object. Programmers can then use this approach to conquer complex page that requires modern UI by dividing them into multiple components and managing them separately without needing to build a single-page application.

Reactivity: Data-Binding and Virtual DOM of Vue

Since each Vue component packs the full features of Vue, it inherits the reactivity system, data binding, and virtual DOM management of Vue.

Reactivity system is one of the reasons why Vue component can turn a boring and static web page into life. It gives the responsiveness and fluidity of a modern web page. Vue brings in some flavor to sections of a Ruby on Rails application that follows conventional routing. It allows us to make an application more interactive and easy to use than your standard resources that you might see from scaffolding a resource in a Rails app.

Wrap-up and the Next Step

We've discussed how to approach a Vue on Rails application from an architecture perspective by demonstrating a few examples. We determined that using a Vue as a first-class citizen approach that uses Webpacker is an ideal scenario and will dive deeper into this approach throughout the book.

There are other features of Vue like validation, internationalization, plugin system, directives, state management, and more. You can also see a list of all the features supported by Vue on Rails at the end of this book.

In the next section, we will examine a way to quickly scaffold Vue component onto Ruby on Rails project and other essential parts of a modern web application.

CHAPTER 3

Model, Vue, and Controller

> *Requirements are not architecture. Requirements are not design, nor are they user interface. Requirements are needs.*
>
> —Hunt and Thomas

This chapter kickstarts your Vue knowledge by covering the essential parts of Vue.js. It starts with the most common Vue features, which are divided into two categories: common core features and tools features. It then transitions to Vue components on Rails project and covers various approaches to passing data within a Vue on Rails project.

The Vue Instance and Other Vue Properties

This section is a look into how we can extend the Rails-first Vue first-class approach to empower Rails views with some independent Vue components. It is not about how we can replace `.vue` files with the `html.erb` files in a Rails project, but rather it should be seen as a way of

B. Lim and R. LaFranchi, *Vue on Rails*, https://doi.org/10.1007/978-1-4842-5116-4_3

41

extending existing Rails architecture and embrace Vue and its components to add some flavor to our applications.

This section aims to cover the Vue instance and its features. The Vue instance is a global JavaScript object the offers everything that Vue framework offers. It is important to start with the lifecycle of a Vue instance to understand how Vue works.

The Vue Lifecycle

Figure 3-1 shows a very good diagram from the Vue documentation (https://vuejs.org/v2/guide/instance.html#Lifecycle-Diagram) that explains the lifecycle of a Vue instance.

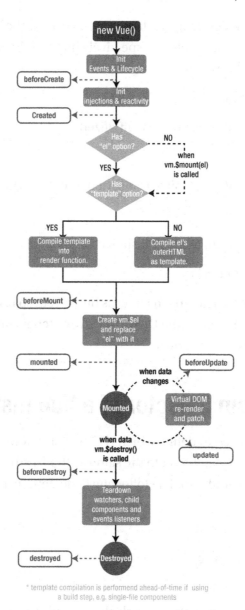

Figure 3-1. *The Vue instance lifecycle (© Yuxi Evan You. Used under the MIT License; see Appendix A)*

There are eight lifecycle hooks that one can use for the Vue instance. Any hook that begins with before respectively happens before the next lifecycle hook. The hooks are:

- beforeCreate

- created – Vue instance is initialized

- beforeMount

- mounted – Vue template is inserted into the DOM

- beforeUpdate

- updated – Data in a Vue instance has changed

- beforeDestroy

- destroyed – The Vue instance is destroyed, so no longer available in the DOM and any watchers or event listeners are torn down.

el – The Main Selector of a Vue Instance

The el property is used to define which HTML element we want to bind the Vue instance to. It can be set to the same as the id attribute of the element we wish to bind it to. The following code demonstrates the use of the el property:

```
Vue.new({
     el: "#identifier"
})
```

In order for the el property to work, there needs to be an html element with the corresponding id attribute such as the following.

```
<div id="identifier"></div>
```

If this reminds you of jQuery's selector, you are not alone. Note that Vue also uses `refs` to select each component. Therefore, you can use `this.$refs.something` to reach out to the "something" component in any .vue file in a Vue on Rails project. In order to access `refs`, it is important to add the `ref` attribute to the components or HTML elements that you need to access as shown here:

```
<div ref="something"></div>
```

Props vs. Data

Props (short for properties) are simply accessible data of the parent components by children components. When a parent's props change, the child's props will change too. The following code declares a prop called something.

```
Vue.component('some-component', {
  props: {
    something: Object
  }
})
```

We can pass down a value to the preceding component in the following HTML where `myObject is a declared object in the parent component`.

```
<some-component :something="myObject"></some-component>
```

Props have the following characteristics:

- One-way binding
- Downwards reactivity (child to parent's property)

The important concept to understand about props is that props enforce one-way data flow from parent to child, so if a child component has the potential to change the value of the prop, the parent will not be aware of the change. In this case it is important to use `vm.$emit`. More info about one-way data flow can be found in the Vue docs at `https://vuejs.org/v2/guide/components-props.html#One-Way-Data-Flow`

Data

Vue's data, as its name suggested, is data residing in any Vue component and can be reused within a `.vue` single-file component. Vue's data has the following characteristics:

- Vue's data is two-way binding.

- Vue's data is reactive (due to binding).

- Vue's data has getter and setters.

The following code demonstrates how to increment a data value.

```
Vue.new({
  data: function() {
    return {
      something: 10
    }
  },
  methods: {
    increment: function() {
      something = this.data.something + 1
    }
  }
})
```

Two-way binding of data attributes is accomplished by using the v-model directive on html input elements, for example:

```
<input type="number" v-model="something"/>
```

Directives

Vue's directives are special markup token on HTML code that acts on DOM elements. Vue has built in directives that you should be familiar with such as the two-way binding helper v-model, but it is important to be aware that it is possible to create your own custom directives. It is similar to HTML attributes. There are four types of directives, namely, empty, literal, multiple, and custom directives.

The directive syntax is as the following:

```
<div v-custom-directive=" "></div>
```

Directives are initialized in JavaScript like so:

```
Vue.directive('custom-directive', {
  inserted: function(el) {
    //...
  }
})
```

Directives are often used when you want to share similar behavior across many HTML elements. An example of a good use case might be when you want to create a custom tooltip or info box applied to different elements. Directives also help with integrating third-party libraries that don't use Vue such as Bootstrap or other libraries that potentially rely on jQuery.

@click – The Method Invoker

The @click event handler provides an easy way to invoke the methods in a Vue instance. The long form is v-on:click. Take the following example of an alert dialog "Hello, Vue" when the button is clicked.

```
<button @click="say_hello">Hello</button>

export default {
  data: function () {
    return {
      message: "Hello something!",
    }
  },
  methods: {
    say_hello: function(e) {
      alert("Hello, Vue")
    }
  }
}
```

Computed Properties, Watchers, and Methods

It is important to understand the difference between computed properties, watchers, and methods. Computed properties are useful for display purposes, for example, if you want to combine two data attributes or compute the sum or average of a list of numbers, where those values might be dynamic. Watchers are defined under the watch property of a Vue instance. A watch method can be defined for each data attribute that we want to track changes for. The following example simply logs the value of the message data attribute every time it changes. It also contains a computed property that calculates the length of the message string. It also includes a click() method which toggles the class list of the element clicked. We will talk a bit more about CSS class and style binding in the next section.

```
<template>
  <div id="" @click="click" ref="something">
    {{ message }} Is {{ messageLength }} characters long
    <input type="text" v-model="message"/>
  </div>
</template>
<script>
export default {
  computed: function () {
    messageLength: function() {
      return this.message.length;
    }
  },
  watch: {
    message: function(val) {
      console.log(val);
    }
  },
  methods: {
    click: function() {
      this.$refs.something.classList.toggle('hello')
    }
  }
}
</script>
```

Class and Style Binding

As its name suggest, we can control the CSS of an HTML element using the style and class attributes. Vue provides a way to use an object for binding CSS class names or CSS to the style attribute where values are props or data variables. For example:

```
<div :style="{width: width + 'px', height: height + 'px'}">
```

This can start to get complicated if you need to bind more than just a couple of style properties. If you are into toggling class/style, I will recommend using toggling a class using this method:

```
<template>
  <div ref="something" @click="click"
       id="app"><p>{{ message }}</p></div>
</template>

<script>
export default {
  data: function () {
    return {
      message: "Hello Vue!"
    }
  },
  methods: {
    click: function() {
      this.$refs.something.classList.toggle('hello')
    }
  }
}
</script>
```

Excessive usage of class and style binding may cause your Vue's data to be bloated. Hence, be sure to namespace your class's or style's data binder. Alternatively, you could simply toggle classes using the `toggleClass()` method provided by vuejs rubygem. It belongs to the vue-on-rails.js library and is demonstrated in the following code.

```
<script>
export default {
  methods: {
    click: function() {
      toggleClass('toggle')
    }
  }
}
</script>
```

Plugins

Vue plugins are great ways to add extra global functionalities to Vue instance. All Vue components will inherit these functionalities. Vue documentation does not recommend overloading the Vue instance and plugins help us to avoid this. The Vuex Rails Plugin is one example of a plugin that the authors have developed to streamline state management as it applies to Rails applications. Usage of the plugin is discussed later in this chapter. We will show basic usage of a generic plugin in the following text.

To use plugins, simply import and use them as shown as follows.

```
import Plugins from 'plugins'
Vue.use(Plugins)
```

If you like to pass in extra options into plugins, you can pass in a hash as options.

```
Vue.use(Plugins, {someOption:true, anotherOption: false})
```

Mixins

Mixins allow us to create reusable functionalities in Vue components. Code gets executed in mixins first before the Vue component's code, so if you define the same method in a component as in the mixin, then the components method will override the mixin's method. They can use the same structure as a Vue component and are great for keeping things DRY (Do not Repeat Yourself). For example, Vue documentation provides a simple example as the following, which simply logs "hello from mixin!" for any component that uses the mixin.[1]

```
// define a mixin object
var myMixin = {
  created: function () {
    this.hello()
  },
  methods: {
    hello: function () {
      console.log('hello from mixin!')
    }
  }
}

// define a component that uses this mixin
var Component = Vue.extend({
  mixins: [myMixin]
})

var component = new Component() // => "hello from mixin!"
```

---

[1] © Yuxi Evan You. Used under the MIT License, see Appendix A.

In the next section, we learn about building independent Vue component and how separation of concerns can assist you in your next Vue on Rails project.

Note   This book does not cover in-depth creation of plugins or mixins. You may read more about the creation of plugins in the Vue documentation at `https://vuejs.org/v2/guide/plugins.html` and `https://vuejs.org/v2/guide/mixins.html`

Building Vue Components

In this section, we will dive into how to integrate Vue components into a Rails application. We will discuss the following topics:

- Component generation using generators from the `vueonrails` gem

- The option to use an x-template as a component template

- Communication between components

- Global and local component registration

Generating Vue Components for Your Vue on Rails Project

The `vueonrails` gem comes packed with helpful generators for creating Vue components in your Vue on Rails project as demonstrated by a simple command.

```
rails g vue something
```

The command generates the following files in your project:

```
create  app/javascript/packs/something.js
create  app/javascript/parts/something/something.vue
create  app/javascript/parts/something/something.js
create  app/javascript/parts/something/something.css
```

Note   You do not need to follow the separation of concern. You would use the option `--single` or `-s` to generate a single-file component with its corresponding pack.

The following command demonstrates the generation of a single-file component:

```
rails g vue something --single
```

The command creates the following files. The `.vue` file encapsulates all the CSS and JS in a single file:

```
create  app/javascript/packs/something.js
create  app/javascript/parts/something.vue
```

Using x-template to Load Your Vue Component

A good way to get started with Vue components in your Rails project is to use an x-template. This eliminates the dependency on Webpacker and having to manage assets in multiple places if your application still depends on the asset pipeline. It is as simple as loading in the CDN link for Vue. For example:

```
<%= javascript_include_tag: "https://cdn.jsdelivr.net/npm/
vue@2.6.10/dist/vue.js" %>
```

In this case, the Vue instance is managed using the asset pipeline, and the template will live in your views.

```
// app/assets/javascripts/pages.js
var XComponent = Vue.component('x-component', {
  template: '#x-component',
  data: function() {
    return {
      message: 'Hello x-template!'
    }
  }
});

// initialize the Vue instance - example that supports
turbolinks
document.addEventListener('turbolinks:load', () => {
  var app = new Vue({
    el: '#app',
    components: { XComponent }
  });
});
```

The template is embedded within a <script> tag with a type attribute that defines it as an x-template. Vue component templates could even be separated out into Rails partials for ease of reuse throughout the application.

```
<!-- app/views/pages/index.html -->

<div id="app">
  <x-component></x-component>
</div>

<script type="text/x-template" id="x-component">
  <div>
```

```
    <p>{{ message }}</p>
  </div>
</script>
```

The downside to using this approach is that you can't take advantage of single-file components and CSS support using Vue loader as well as taking advantage of a modular approach with Webpacker. Using x-template is a good way to get started with Vue in legacy Rails applications by using the existing asset pipeline. For new projects, we recommend using Webpacker from the start.

Communication Between Vue Components in a Rails Project

The concept of one-way down communication between parent and child components is an important concept to grasp, which we previously discussed. However, what if you need to communicate a change to a component that doesn't have this direct relationship? That task is not as trivial. Also, how does this apply to a Rails environment?

Let's take the example of flash alerts in Rails. Typically, flash notices and alerts are set on the server using `flash[:notice]` = `'Notice'` and the template for these alerts live in partial and rendered on the server side if any notices exist. In the situation where flash is used widely throughout an existing application, we can create a Vue instance that supports this as well.

Let's say we want to create a toast notification that can be called from any Vue component with the app. This example will use a few simple buttons that live in a separate Vue instance and will demonstrate how a server-side flash can also be displayed on page load.

Webpacker will be used to take advantage of CSS support, and the instance will be appended to the document body.

```
// app/javascript/parts/flash/flash.vue
<template>
  <div id="flash">
    <div class="toast" v-for="message in messages"
    :class="[message[0]]">
      <p>{{ message[1] }}</p>
    </div>
  </div>
</template>
```

Flash messages can be rendered from the server on data attributes and can be called when the flash component is mounted.

```
<div id="flashData"
     data-notice="<%= flash[:notice] %>"
     data-error="<%= flash[:error] %>"
     data-warning="<%= flash[:warning] %>">
</div>
<!-- or by using a content tag -->
<%= content_tag "div", nil, id: "flashData", data: {
  notice: flash[:notice],
  error: flash[:error],
  warning: flash[:warning]
} %>

// app/javascript/parts/flash/flash.js

export default {
  data: function() {
    return {
      messages: [],
      counter: 0
    }
  },
```

```
mounted() {
  var flashFromServer = document.getElementById('flashData');
  this.notice(flashFromServer.dataset.notice);
  this.error(flashFromServer.dataset.error);
  this.warn(flashFromServer.dataset.warning);
},
methods: {
  notice(msg) {
    this.toastMsg('notice', msg)
  },
  error(msg) {
    this.toastMsg('error', msg)
  },
  warn(msg) {
    this.toastMsg('warning', msg)
  },
  toastMsg(type, msg) {
    this.counter++
    this.messages.push([type, `${msg} (#${this.counter})`])
    var vm = this
    setTimeout(function() {
      vm.messages.shift()
    }, 3000)
  }
}
};
```

Now, for any component within our application, we can access the component's methods directly by defining the instance globally on the window.

```
// definition in the entry point
var FlashVM = new Vue(Flash)
window.FlashVM = FlashVM

// usage
FlashVM.notice('Notice')
```

There are alternatives for communication between components such as using a global event bus. This method consists of having a single Vue instance that is responsible for emitting and receiving messages.

```
// receiver in another component
  EventBus.$on('flash', function(data) {
    this.notice(data.message)
  })

// emitter from one component
  EventBus.$emit('flash', { message: 'Notice' })
```

Another option is to use a global event listener.

```
//receiver
  var vm = this
  document.addEventListener('receive', function() {
    vm.interesting()
  }, false)

//emitter
  var event = document.createEvent('Event')
  event.initEvent('receive', true, true)
  document.dispatchEvent(event)
```

The event bus and listener options can quickly make the application fairly convoluted with a more complex application. In this scenario, using Vuex may be a better solution for more robust state management.

Registering Components

In this section we will take a look at two methods for registering components, namely, global and local registration.

Global Registration of Component

Registering a component globally means that the resultant global component is accessible by all of the other components. This is accomplished through the Vue.component method.

```
import ComponentName from 'component.vue'
Vue.component('component-tag', ComponentName) // <component-tag>
```

Local Registration of Component

Registering a component locally means it is only accessible by the local components and its children only.

```
<template>
  <component-tag></component-tag>
</template>

import ComponentName from 'component.vue'

export default {

components: {'component-tag': ComponentName}

}
```

Passing Data from Vue to Server

This section will discuss how to pass data from the Vue frontend to the server in the most effective way with a focus on developer happiness.

If you are using Rails view, without .vue, you can still embed v-model into Rails view, and they will work fine. This is provided if you follow the setup found in Chapter 2.

To submit data from the Vue side to the server side, we can use an HTML form to submit a post request. In the next example, we will use a form component to generate a HTML component. The form component is called vue_form_for.

Note   The vueonrails gem ships with a form component in the form of plugins called vue-form-for available at http://github.com/vueonrails/vue-form-for. It is inspired by Rails' view helper to generate HTML forms. To see how to use vue-form-for, read on.

The following shows an example of vue-form-for usage.

```
import FormFor from 'vue-form-for'
Vue.use(FormFor)

<!- Use this in .vue files -->
<form-for>
  <label-tag for="name"/>
  <text-field for="name"/>
  <submit-tag/>
</form-for>
```

You can also use v-model in Rails form by doing the following:

```
<%= form.text_field :something, ':value': "textfield" %>
```

This generates an input form that has a binding to the <textfield> variable inside Vue instance.

The `vueonrails` gem provides an option to include a form when generating a component demonstrated by the following command:

```
vue g somecomponent --form
```

With HTTP Client

Another way to send data from the Vue side to the server side is using a HTTP client. Writing ES6 gives you shorter function syntax and binding to this. The new function syntax is called the arrow function.

```
axios.get(this.onComponentMountedURL)
  .then((response) => {
    this.onComponentMounted = response
})

var application_instance = this
  if(application_instance.onComponentUpdatedURL != ""){
    axios.get(application_instance.onComponentUpdatedURL)
    .then(function (response) {
      application_instance.onComponentUpdatedURL = response
    })
}
```

A shorter and lighter `axios` request is helpful when you need to sprinkle `axios` requests throughout your Vue components.

Most Vue components request data loading at the beginning. Use the `vue-autorequest` plugin to further trim off those loading requests of your every Vue-component, making your components less bloated. To get started, simply register the plugin using the following.

```
import AutoRequest from 'vue-autorequest'
Vue.use(AutoRequest)
```

And the following demonstrates usage of vue-autorequest within a component:

```
<script>
export default {

   data(): function(){
  return {
    onComponentCreatedURL: "" //set the url here #1
  }
},
  watch: {
   onComponentCreated(response){
     // receive data from here
    }
  }
}
</script>
```

Note   Together with base components, vue-autorequest is imported automatically when the vueonrails gem is included in the Gemfile. Run the rails vue:setup to complete the initialization.

Retiring vue-resource and Using Axios

Since Vue 2.0, the Vue team has stopped recommending vue-resource as the default HTTP client. Instead, axios has been picked because it provides a very simple API for making HTTP requests. Therefore, we recommend using axios over vue-resource for your Vue on Rails project.

Axios is created by Matt Zabriskie, and the Vue core team has recommended axios as the HTTP client for Vue.js.

In the next section, we discuss how to route a Rails project with a vue-router. There is an example project to demonstrate the capability of vue-router.

Routing with Vue Router within a Rails Project

You may download a copy of the Vue Router with Rails-API from `http://github.com/TBA/TBA`. This section covers how to use Vue Router within a Rails project. Vue Router is the Vue way of routing HTTP request in a project generated using vue-cli.

In this book, we choose to favor the Rails router over Vue Router in a Vue on Rails project. The benefits are listed in Chapter 2. We would like to provide an example of using Vue Router for those who may decide on taking the SPA route or at least help in the process of choosing an architecture for an application.

We will demonstrate how you would translate routes for a blog application (e.g., defining resources :posts in your `config.rb file`) to Vue Router. You can start by creating a new app, adding the `vue-router` npm package, and running the scaffold.

```
rails new vue_router --webpack=vue
cd vue_router
yarn add vue-router
yarn install

rails generate scaffold post title:string body:text --api
rails db:migrate
```

This setup will require the root path to point to a single file, but all of the HTML will be handled by Vue components and routing, and redirects will be handled on the client side by the Vue Router.

Create an index.html file that includes the default Javascript pack for Vue (<%= javascript_pack_tag "hello_vue" %>) and point root to this route.

```
# config/routes.rb
root to: "posts#index"
```

Creating the Router File

The router file will live in app/javascripts/router.js and will contain the configuration required for Vue Router. One problem with Vue Router is that there aren't any conventions followed for defining typical routes in a similar manner to the Rails resources method. Each route will need to be defined individually, but we will try to follow Rails conventions.

Under Rails' conventions, a route will be defined for the posts index, show, new, and edit routes, and corresponding components will live in the app/javascripts/posts folder.

```
import VueRouter from 'vue-router'
import Posts from 'posts/Posts'
import Post from 'posts/Post'
import NewPost from 'posts/NewPost'
import EditPost from 'posts/EditPost'

const routes = [
  { path: '/posts', component: Posts },
  { path: '/posts/new', component: NewPost },
  { path: '/posts/:id', component: Post, name: 'post' },
  { path: '/posts/:id/edit', component: EditPost, name: 'edit_
  post' }
]
```

```
const router = new VueRouter({
  routes
})
```

```
export default router
```

Initializing vue-router

vue-router is imported and initialized in our pack file along with the configuration defined previously.

```
import Vue from 'vue'
import VueRouter from 'vue-router'
Vue.use(VueRouter)
```

```
import router from '../router'
import App from '../app.vue'
```

```
document.addEventListener('DOMContentLoaded', () => {
  const el = document.body.appendChild(document.
createElement('hello'))
  const app = new Vue({
    el,
    router,
    render: h => h(App)
  })

  console.log(app)
})
```

This makes the router instance available throughout the application as this.$router which allows for dynamic routing. This will also make this.$route available which is important for accessing route parameters, which we will discuss further. Make sure to look at the official documentation [1] to discover Vue's routing capabilities.

We need to make sure to insert the `<router-view>` tag appropriately. In the example, we insert it into `app.vue`, but in a more robust application, you will need to think about the template of your application and where to place them.

```
<template>
  <div id="app">
    <router-view></router-view>
  </div>
</template>
```

In the example, we don't have a base route defined (/), so our app component immediately redirects to the posts path when created. `this.$router.push()` is used to dynamically change routes. This is basically equivalent to the Rails method `redirect_to`.

```
created: function () {
  this.$router.push('/posts')
}
```

Using `<router-link>`

`<router-link>` is the equivalent of `link_to` in Ruby on Rails. The tag only requires a to attribute which can take the path of the route or an object containing other information such as the name of the route and parameters.

In our Post component, we can demonstrate how to link to different routes with or without parameters. The Read More and Edit links require an id as a parameter.

```
<template>
  <ul>
    <li v-for="post in posts">
```

```
    {{ post.title }}
    <router-link :to="{ name: 'post', params: { id: post.id
    }}">Read More</router-link>
    | <router-link :to="{ name: 'edit_post', params: { id:
    post.id }}">Edit</router-link>
    | <a href="#!" @click.prevent="deletePost(post)">
    Delete</a>
  </li>
  <li>
    <router-link to="/posts/new">New Post</router-link>
  </li>
</ul>
</template>
```

Routing Parameters

Accessing routing parameter is simple. As discussed before, we have access to this.$route. Parameters are accessed simply through this.$route.params.

For example, in our Post component, we want to fetch the content for a particular post id and similarly when editing an existing post. We can do this when the component is mounted using axios. In our example, http is an instance of axios.

```
mounted: function () {
  var vm = this
  http.get(`/posts/${this.$route.params.id}.json`)
    .then(function (res) {
      vm.post = res.data
    })
```

```
    .catch(function (err) {
      alert(err)
    })
}
```

Redirect or Alert

In Ruby on Rails projects, when a form is submitted it's common to redirect on a successful response or render when a model's validations do not pass.

In our example using Vue Router, the client side interacts with the Rails backend using JSON endpoints, so we don't have access to redirects or rendering, just response status codes and JSON responses.

So a form submission for a new post will need to handle any errors on the client side. In the example, we will simply alert the error response in case it happens. In a robust application, you will want to inform your users in a more visually appealing manner, such as a bootstrap alert or other methods.

On a successful creation of a new post, we simply redirect to the path for the created post using this.$router.push(). Here is the full example of our NewPost component.

```
<template>
  <div>
    <h1>New Post</h1>
    <form @submit.prevent="createPost()">
      <label for="title">Title</label>
      <input type="text" v-model="post.title" name="title"
      id="title">
      <label for="body">Body</label>
      <textarea name="body" id="body" v-model="post.body">
      </textarea>
```

```
      <input type="submit" value="Save Post">
    </form>
    <router-link to="/posts">&laquo; Back to Posts</router-link>
  </div>
</template>

<script>
import http from '../http'
export default {
  data: function() {
    return {
      post: {
        title: ",
        body: "
      }
    }
  },
  methods: {
    createPost: function() {
      var vm = this
      http.post('/posts.json', { post: this.post })
        .then(function(res) {
          vm.$router.push(`/posts/${res.data.id}`)
        })
        .catch(function(err) {
          alert(err)
        })
    }
  }
}
</script>
```

Since it is a new post that we are creating, we actually can't route to it until it is successfully created. We use the id from the response to include in our route. If an error occurs (response code of 4XX or 5XX), then we alert the response in the browser.

Points to Ponder

We will not be using Vue Router in Vue on Rails projects. Continuing to use Rails routing allows us to maintain the conventions of Rails and stick with a traditional MVC pattern. This allows us to be more flexible with Vue and use it in scenarios or in particular controllers where it makes sense. Using Rails router also promotes many battle-tested strategies in Rails view like Rails Helpers, Partial, etc.

All in all, Rails router allows for better performance in a Vue on Rails project, in contrast to a single-page application (SPA). With an SPA, it results in bloated asset files, but a particular page or view may only need a small portion of the code loaded.

In the next section, this book will explore controlling state of a Rails view using Vuex, a simple state management plugin for Vue.

Managing State of a Rails View Using Vuex

This section demonstrates the usage of Vuex – a state management system on Vue components inside a Rails project.

You see, component's data is the key that open doors between individual and independent components. As you build bigger apps, data between each component parts become important. The simplest data management is in the form of an empty hash.

```
var data = {}
```

But as the data grows bigger, you want to have an easy way to control this `variable data` that has transformed into `variable bigger_data`.

Vuex is the recommended heavy-weight solution to manage your data between each Vue component as your data gets bigger and messier.

Introduction

States are representations of the app at different timing. This means that managing states or having a good strategy to deal with them can be very useful in making your modern web application.

The Trouble with Vuex and Other State Management Tools

Most state management tools are just bloated with theory and heavy-laden principle like the single source of truth (SSOT). SSOT sounds poetic on paper, but a technology is usually not meant for long-term programmers' happiness or pragmatic approach. Design patterns used around central state management tend to be convoluted and hard to understand for those not familiar with the concept, so it makes it a tough learning curve for most. Taking Vuex for example, to be able to change, you need to define a getter, an action, and a mutation.

Why Should We Manage States?

States are also relevant when each component talks to each other. States are important for communication as

- A temporary data representation of a component

- A useful communication channel among components

- Persistent storage of the data presentation among components

The point about persistent storage is controversial as one may argue a database is a better tool to be doing that. This is why Stimulus is taking a different approach when comes to state management. Stimulus takes the states and attaches them onto the HTML elements. This approach means that Stimulus does not manage states but continuously replaces the entire HTML with the baked-in states of the web component.

The DOM is also centralized and singular. The difference is that a state manager stores numbers and string in a neatly organized way for programmers, while a DOM's sole purpose is to display design on the web with a secondary purpose to represent states.

For instance, consider a clinic counter; clicking the count button will increment the number by one. Each action causes the representative to increment, thereby reflected in the displayed number. Simple and elegant.

Do you really need Vuex or any of the state management all the time? Is there an easier way to deal with states? Ruby on Rails will be shipping stimulus.js which abandons state management entirely by storing all the states in the HTML itself. We will provide an overview of using Vuex in a Vue on Rails project and lead into a plugin that we have developed to abstract away a lot of the concepts and to make it easier to hook Vuex into the Rails backend by following conventions.

Getting Started with Vuex

Let's start by installing Vuex:

```
yarn add vuex
```

If you are using the vuejs gem, the installation is done for you. The following shows you how to **scaffold a Vue component with Vuex:**

```
vue generate <component_name> --vuex
```

Note   The `vueonrails` gem ships with the `vuex-rails-plugin` that offers a painless mapping of Rails resources to Vuex modules.

Vuex Rails Plugin

Vuex is often not very trivial to use for developers who are not familiar with similar state management tools and is a hard problem to get right. The Vuex Rails plugins attempts to simplify this problem for developers and easily maps Rails resources to Vuex state and abstracts away common code that is created when using Vuex.

The plugin works well if Rails conventions are followed particularly when resources are scaffolded and supported a JSON format. A more in-depth example of using the plugin can be found in our hands-on tutorial for the Tic Tac Toe app in Chapter 5. Here we can demonstrate simple usage.

Configuring the Plugin

A plugin needs to be initialized for each resource that you want to map, so for example if you have posts and categories defined as resources in Rails, then it can be initialized like so.

```
// store.js
import Vuex from 'vuex'
import Vue from 'vue'
Vue.use(Vuex)
import VuexRailsPlugin from 'vuex-rails-plugin/src/
VuexRailsPlugin'

export default new Vuex.Store({
  // ...
  plugins: [
```

```
    VuexRailsPlugin('posts'),
    VuexRailsPlugin('categories')
  ]
})
```

Start Using Vuex Rails Plugins

Under the hood, the Vuex Rails plugin allows you to call common CRUD actions from your Vue components and performs a lot of the grunt work such as making the web request to the backend and mutating Vuex state appropriately to keep in sync with the backend.

A simple example is fetching a list of posts or calling the posts#index action. Vuex actions and state can be used inside components using mapState and mapActions.

```
// posts.vue
<template>
  <ul>
    <li v-for="post in posts">{{ post.title }}</li>
  </ul>
</template>

<script>
import { mapState, mapActions } from 'vuex'
export default {
  // ...
  created() {
    this.getPosts({ page: 1, limit: 10 }) // ex. with
    parameters
  },
  computed: {
    ...mapState('posts', {
      posts: state => state.all
```

```
    })
  },
  methods: {
    ...mapActions('posts', {
      getPosts: 'getAll' // possible actions - getAll, get,
      create, update, destroy
    })
  }
}
</script>
```

See the README for `vuex-rails-plugin` showing all actions that are supported (`https://github.com/rlafranchi/vuex-rails-plugin`). The plugin may not solve problems for more complex state management, but it still works side by side with Vuex, so you can always create custom Vuex modules, actions, mutations, etc.

The next section discusses handling scenarios that need data in a real-time or near real-time manner and will cover polling and using Action Cable.

Passing Data from Server to Vue

This section focuses on passing data and information from the server to the Vue frontend or your Vue components inside a Rails project. Sometimes, your web application requires real-time or frequent updates to its interface. This will require you to push the data from the server to the frontend. In this section, we will explore two ways to pass data from server to Vue: Action Cable and simple polling.

Also, check out the hands-on tutorial on Action Cable of Vue on Rails in Chapter 5 where you learn to create a two-player, real-time game.

Using Action Cable as a push technology

Another method is to use Action Cable like web-socket to push data from the server side to the Vue side of things. There will be a full example of Action Cable in our Chapter 5 hands-on tutorial. We will show the basics here on how to install and configure Action Cable on the frontend and backend.

On the frontend, we can add the `actioncable` package to our installed packages.

```
yarn add actioncable
```

An easy way to get Action Cable working with Vue is to initialize the consumer as a Vue prototype in your entry point, which allows us to use cable within our Vue components as `this.$cable`. By default, Rails serves Action Cable sockets at the `/cable` path.

```
import Vue from 'vue'
import App from '../app.vue'
import ActionCable from 'actioncable'
Vue.prototype.$cable = ActionCable.createConsumer('/cable')
```

Now in our app we can subscribe to the appropriate channel for our component.

```
// app.vue
export default {
  data: function () {
    return {
      message: 'Waiting for messages...'
    }
  },
  created: function () {
    const vm = this
```

```
this.$cable.subscriptions.create(
  { channel: 'NotificationsChannel' },
  {
    received: function (data) {
      vm.message = data.message
    }
  }
);
}
}
```

Action Cable is supported out of the box on the Rails backend, so it is just a matter of creating a channel for broadcasting messages.

```
class NotificationsChannel < ApplicationCable::Channel
  def subscribed
    stream_from "notifications_channel"
  end
end

#For instance
ActionCable.server.broadcast "notifications_channel", message:
"Hello ActionCable!"
```

A Simple Polling

Last, but not least, a simple polling will be a good way to keep data in sync from the Vue side to server side. This is not a push technology or a Javascript hack but a consistent request to the endpoint for new data.

```
<script>
  function doWork(){
    console.log("doing work")
  }
```

```
setInterval(doWork, 1000) //every 1000 miliseconds
</script>
```

Note   setInterval() needs to be cleared using clearInterval() when a Vue component is destroyed; otherwise a new interval will be created each time that a component is initialized causing potential performance problems.

Wrap-up and the Next Step

In this chapter we learned about the basics of Vue and the Vue lifecycle, Vue components, how to route your Vue on Rails application, using Vuex for state management, and passing data between Rails and Vue. In the next part, this book will explore some real-world hands-on tutorials. You will get to integrate Action Cable, active storage, nested form, and specific-page Vue of a Vue on Rails project. The first chapter in the next part starts with some short tutorials. Let's go.

PART II

Hands on the Wheels – Tutorials

Chapter 4. Real-World Applications Through Short Tutorials

Chapter 5. Making a Real-Time Two-Player Game with Action Cable

Chapter 6. Building an Image-Cropping Tool with Vue and Active Storage

CHAPTER 4

Real-World Applications Through Short Tutorials

I also really care about the approachability part of Vue, which is rooted in the belief that technology should be enabling more people to build things

—Evan You

We learn best by learning through examples. In this chapter, we provide real-world examples to illustrate certain points.

The `vueonrails` gem comes with Ruby and JavaScript methods that allow us to enable a concept that we like to call specific-page Vue. We will demonstrate how to use specific-page Vue with and without Turbolinks in the first tutorial.

We previously discussed `form-for` Vue helpers and will dive deeper into its usage as it applies to nested forms in the second tutorial in this chapter and how we can tie our forms into the backend. We will then investigate certain topics like configuration using application template, Vue-UI compatibility, internationalization, simple state management, and even server-side rendering.

© Bryan Lim and Richard LaFranchi 2019
B. Lim and R. LaFranchi, *Vue on Rails*, https://doi.org/10.1007/978-1-4842-5116-4_4

> **Note**   As mentioned earlier in the book, source code for most code
> examples and tutorials is available at the vueonrails organizational
> GitHub account at `https://github.com/vueonrails/code-`
> `examples`. You can also reach out to the authors, Bryan (`http://`
> `github.com/ytbryan`) or Richard (`https://github.com/`
> `rlafranchi`).

Specific-Page Vue Inside Rails Products

Specific-page Vue allows developers to choose a specific Vue component
to display on a specific Rails view. Similar to page-specific JavaScript
that executes JavaScript for each page as if it behaves like a single-page
application (SPA), a specific-page Vue (SPV) executes its Vue component
and its corresponding JavaScript on a page much the same way.

The javascript_pack_tag for application.js is where all your component
packs can be consolidated and delivered onto your Rails view. It is the
new asset pipeline for your Rails product, therefore treating it as the single
pipeline.

Rails 6 will ship with a single `javascript_pack_tag as the default`
`javascript` pipeline on the main `app/views/layout/application.`
`html.erb`. javascript_pack_tag is responsible to import each Vue
components into the final Rails application.

```
<%= javascript_pack_tag 'application','data-turbolinks-track':
'reload' %>
```

The alternative to SPV is to sprinkle Webpacker `javascript_pack_tag`
on each Rails view. This will result in multiple `javascript_pack_tag`
instances on multiple Rails views.

```
<%= javascript_pack_tag 'component' %>
```

SPV on Rails is a refuge to the SPA exodus that you may be having in your company. An SPA has the unhealthy constraint on small business and small team where the JavaScript application is loaded once and gain full responsibility of what happens next throughout the entire web app lifecycle.

The following highlights the difficulty of the SPA approach:

- Budget required for frontend and backend dichotomy which contributes to a larger starting team size, usually at an early stage of the product lifecycle.

- The complexity of SPA isn't worthwhile for most projects. This is especially so if you are working in a small- to medium-sized team.

- Dividing teams into frontend and backend creates siloes that tend not to retain cross-functional knowledge.

- It is far more laborious to build a robust SPA than a monolithic SPV on Rails app due to bigger required team and unnecessary overhead in code.

The following highlights the proposition of specific-page Vue with monolithic Rails architecture:

- Smaller team required to ship a majestic monolithic Rails with SPV and single-file components.

- Scalable approach towards completion of final product.

  - The Vue components/parts are sprinkled across the Rails views.

- Scalability depends on completion of components instead of completion of entire frontend or backend.

- Large components can be broken down into multiple smaller components using single-file components.

While single-page application dominates the mind space of the frontend development, many developers have come out to discuss that a monolithic application is easier to manage. Can we ship with something that behaves like page-specific application while enjoying the MVC clean separation of concerns? We would like to propose the SPV approach which allows us to get the benefits of an SPA such as a responsive and reactive UX. In this scenario we can choose where we want to incorporate Vue.

Specific-Page Vue

Let's start off with an empty Rails project by running the following application template:

```
rails new app --webpack=vue
```

Note   You will need to add vueonrails and Webpacker inside Gemfile. Run `bundle exec bundle install` to get all its dependencies.

The following assumes that we have already set up a Rails project using the tools that we have previously mentioned. We can generate a component and modify the entry point slightly. The following code demonstrates an entry point or a pack tag that initializes an SPV. It only loads the Vue instance on the `pages/index.html` view.

```
import Vue from 'vue'
import App from '../parts/something/tab_component.vue'
import {isView} from 'vueonrails'

document.addEventListener('DOMContentLoaded', () => {
  if(isView('pages#index')){
    document.body.appendChild(document.createElement('hello'))
    const app = new Vue({
      render: h => h(App)
    }).$mount('hello')
    console.log({app})
  }
})
```

Make note of the isView() function; this is a helper method provided by the vueonrails gem that allows us to load a Vue instance only on specific pages. Let's say we have a different instance that we want to load on the pages/second.html view. We can also add the following to the same pack file:

```
if(isView('pages#second)){
    document.body.appendChild(document.createElement('hello'))
    const app = new Vue({
      render: h => h(App)
    }).$mount('hello')
    console.log({app})
}
```

In order for SPV to work, the application.html.erb layout file needs to be modified appropriately to add a class to the body of the layout. For this, we can use the specific_page_vue helper and modify the body tag appropriately.

```erb
<%= content_tag :body, class: specific_page_vue do %>
  <%= yield %>
<% end %>
```

Here is the full content of the application.html.erb layout file

```erb
<!DOCTYPE html>
<html>
  <head>
    <title>SpecificPageVue</title>
    <%= csrf_meta_tags %>
    <%= csp_meta_tag %>

    <%= stylesheet_link_tag    'application', media: 'all',
    'data-turbolinks-track': 'reload' %>
    <%= javascript_include_tag 'application', 'data-turbolinks-
    track': 'reload' %>

    <%= javascript_pack_tag 'application', 'data-turbolinks-
    track': 'reload' %>

  </head>

  <%= content_tag :body, class: specific_page_vue do %>
    <%= yield %>
  <% end %>
</html>
```

This example assumes that //= require "turbolinks" was removed from the application.js file. In order for Turbolinks to work with SPV, we need to make some small changes which is demonstrated in the next section.

Specific-Page Vue with Turbolinks

Specific-page Vue works great with the Turbolinks. This section uses the same layout file that we showed in the previous section and assumes you have Turbolinks installed. Make sure that Turbolinks is loaded in the application.js file.

```
//= require turbolinks
```

In order for Turbolinks to work with Vue, we need to install the vue-turbolinks package.

```
yarn add vue-turbolinks
```

Create a Turbolinks-compatible tab component.

```
import Vue from 'vue/dist/vue.esm'
import App from '../parts/tab_component/tab_component.vue'
import Tabs from 'vue-tabs-component';
import {isView} from 'vueonrails'
import TurbolinksAdapter from 'vue-turbolinks'
Vue.use(Tabs);
Vue.use(TurbolinksAdapter)

document.addEventListener('turbolinks:load', () => {
  if(isView('pages#index')){
    document.body.appendChild(document.createElement('hello'))
    const app = new Vue({
      render: h => h(App)
    }).$mount('hello')
    console.log({app})
  }
})
```

Create a second Turbolinks-compatible tab component.

```
import Vue from 'vue/dist/vue.esm'
import App from '../parts/table/table.vue'
import {isView} from 'vueonrails'
import TurbolinksAdapter from 'vue-turbolinks'
Vue.use(TurbolinksAdapter)

document.addEventListener('turbolinks:load', () => {
  if(isView('pages#second')){
    document.body.appendChild(document.createElement('hello'))
    const app = new Vue({
      render: h => h(App)
    }).$mount('hello')
    console.log({app})
  }
})
```

The important difference to note between using Turbolinks is that Turbolinks listens for the `turbolinks:load` event where normally without Turbolinks we would use the `DOMContentLoaded` event. Turbolinks offers the benefit of avoiding page loads in the browser and seamless transitions between pages. This allows us to create a great user experience in the transition between pages in our Rails products that use Vue and those that don't.

Nested Form with form-for Component

vue-form-for is a Vue component that mimics the `form-for` and `form-with` of Rails. It generates HTML form code that makes it possible to post forms to the Rails backend. A Vue form component enables reactivity and has better integration with other Vue libraries like Vuex, Vue UI, or Vue devtool. Form-for uses XMLHttpRequest to request data, and this means there is no other HTTP dependencies like axios.

<form-for> adds Vue-powered forms into Rails architecture. How do we created nested attributes to create advanced forms in modern Rails?

In this section, we will use form-for to create nested forms to submit a list of student names and the subjects they are taking. A nested form is one that accepts two models or more.

First, we generate our first model student:

```
rails g scaffold student name:string
```

Then let's generate a second model subject:

```
rails g model subjects name:string subject_id:integer
student:references
```

Note that we are using reference for classroom. This will be useful for database relationship and migration of data.

Next, let's edit the model association as shown in the following code:

```
class Student < ApplicationRecord
  has_many :subjects
  accepts_nested_attributes_for :subjects
end

class Subjects < ApplicationRecord
  belongs_to :student, optional: true
end
```

Let's create a Vue form using form-for, label-tag, text-field, and submit-tag:

```
<template>
  <form-for model="student">
    <div class="field">
      <label-tag for="name">Name</label-tag>
```

```
        <text-field for="name"></text-field>
    </div>

    <fields-for model="subjects" >
        <label-tag for="name">Subject</label-tag>
        <text-field for="name"></text-field>
    </fields-for>

    <div class="actions">
      <submit-tag></submit-tag>
    </div>
  </form-for>
</template>
```

Next, let's update our student controller:

```
# controllers/student_controller.rb
def new
  @student = Student.new
  @student.subjects.build
end
...
private
def show_params
  params.require(:show).permit(:name,
    :students_attributes => [:name]
  )
end

<template>
  <form-for model="">
    <fields-for model="<%= @something %>">
      <text-field for="name">
      <text-field for="address">
```

</fields-for>
</form-for>
</template>

Now, here's the part where we will be tempted to use the erb form.
If you switch to Vue component, you will have better integration with
other Vue libraries. In Figure 4-1, the Vue Devtool shows that Vue 2.6.10 is
detected and the FormFor component is displayed.

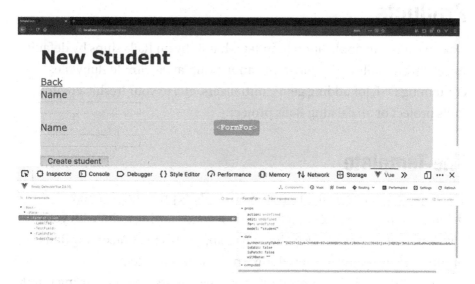

Figure 4-1. *Using the Vue Devtool with Firefox browser 67.0.4*

The full project can be downloaded from GitHub by running the
following command:

```
git clone http://github.com/ytbryan/simple_form
bundle exec bundle install
bundle exec rails server
```

Optionally, you can speed up the rendering of your Vue component by running the webpack-dev-server in your development environment. Open another tab in your terminal and run the following command:

```
./bin/webpack-dev-server
```

Application Template of Vue on Rails Products

Next, we have an application template that Ruby on Rails ships by default. According to Rails' guide, an application template is simple Ruby files containing DSL for adding gems, initializers, etc. to your freshly created Rails project or an existing Rails project.

The Template

The application template jump starts your Rails product with new default and popular tools that gives you a good starting point with your development process. It also allows developers to customize your Rails products to be ready for everything what Vue has to offer.

Such automatic customization gives developers a better starting point and helps to skip mind-numbing configuration of Jest test, single file component, simple state management, Vue UI, internationalization, and even server-side rendering which we will explore in this chapter.

An example of the application template that is designed for latest Webpacker and Vue can be found at `https://github.com/vueonrails/vueonrails/blob/master/lib/installs/setup.rb`

Add the following code to the Gemfile and run bundle exec bundle install:

```
gem 'vueonrails'
```

To complete the setup via the Vue on Rails application template, run the following command at the terminal:

```
rails vue:setup
```

Options of Vue on Rails Application Template

The following sections describe some optional tools that you can enable when invoking the application template. You can enable the tools by passing in some options during invocation. For example, `rails new app -m="https://vueonrails.com/vue" --option` where `--option` is the preset option name. By default, these options are disabled to ship you a lightweight default setting.

Administrate

Administrate is a Rails engine that adds powerful admin dashboard to your Rails product. With Administrate, you can manage your data and models at the backend with ease. This option will install Administrate as the default admin system for your Vue on Rails projects.

The full command is

```
Rails new app --m="https://vueonrails.com/vue" --admin
```

Whenever

Whenever is a scheduler for your Cron job. With Whenever, you can run your tasks in a timely fashion. This option will install Whenever as the default automated system for your Vue on Rails projects.

The full command is

```
rails new app --m="https://vueonrails.com/vue" --whenever
```

Bootstrap

Bootstrap is a popular style framework for web application. Your Rails product will be styled with in a professional outlook. This option will install bootstrap as the default template for your Vue on Rails projects.

The full command is

```
rails new app --m="https://vueonrails.com/vue" --bootstrap
```

Foundation

Foundation is a frontend framework for web application. Foundation styles your rails products in a professional way. This option will install foundation as the default template for your Vue on Rails projects.

The full command is

```
rails new app --m https://vueonrails.com/vue --foundation
```

Font Awesome

Font Awesome is an icon and font toolkit based on CSS and LESS. Your rails products will look more professional with the icons and fonts from Font Awesome. This option will install Font Awesome as the default template for your Vue on Rails projects.

The full command is

```
rails new app --m https://vueonrails.com/vue --fontawesome
```

Sidekiq

Sidekiq is a popular background progressing system. You can process thousands of jobs and tasks easily with Sidekiq. This option will install Sidekiq as the default background worker for your Vue on Rails projects.

The full command with Sidekiq is

```
rails new app --m https://vueonrails.com/vue --sidekiq
```

Devise

Devise is an authentication system for Rails products. Devise saves you time to setup the authentication and authorization system in your Rails products. This option will install devise as the authentication system for your Vue on Rails projects.

The full command with Devise option is

```
rails new app --m https://vueonrails.com/vue --devise
```

Livereload

Livereload is an auto-refresher for your web application. With Livereload, the browser gets refreshed when you save a file. This option will install Livereload as a development auto-refresher for your Vue on Rails projects.

The full command with Livereload option is

```
rails new app --m https://vueonrails.com/vue --livereload
```

Vue UI Compatibility in Rails Products

Vue UI is the official graphical interface to create, manage, and develop Vue projects. While we are shipping Rails products, we can leverage on Vue UI to better manage our Vue dependencies before releasing the final product into production. Figure 4-2 shows the Vue UI with a list of project JavaScript dependencies.

Figure 4-2. *The project dependencies of Vue UI. You can manage, update, install, or remove your Vue and Javascript dependencies within the project dependencies*

Figure 4-3 shows the Vue UI with the project tasks.

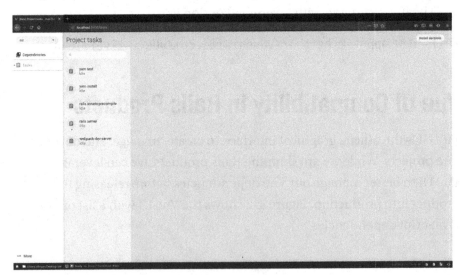

Figure 4-3. *The task page of Vue UI. You can execute or stop project tasks. Vue on Rails gem ships with five default project tasks. One of the tasks is to start the Rails server from Vue UI.*

The Vue UI support is enabled when the developer run the vue:setup or when they invoke the application template with the -m option

Manual Enabling of Vue UI in Rails Products

Sometimes, you may wish to have fine control over the codes that are added into your project. This means developers want to manually add the configuration code instead of relying on an automatic generator.

To enable Vue UI manually, simply add the following configuration code to the package.json at the root project of your Rails product.

```
"scripts": {
  "yarn test": "jest",
  "yarn install": "yarn install --check-files",
  "rails assets:precompile": "yarn install --check-files;
  rails assets:precompile",
  "rails server": "rails server",
  "webpack-dev-server": "./bin/webpack-dev-server"
},
"jest": {
  "moduleFileExtensions": [
    "js",
    "vue"
  ],
  "moduleNameMapper": {
    "^@/(.*)$": "<rootDir>/app/javascript/parts/$1"
  },
  "transform": {
    "^.+\\.js$": "<rootDir>/node_modules/babel-jest",
    ".*\\.(vue)$": "<rootDir>/node_modules/vue-jest"
  },
```

```
  "transformIgnorePatterns": [
    "node_modules/(?!(vueonrails)/)"
  ],
  "testPathIgnorePatterns": [
    "<rootDir>/config/webpack/"
  ],
  "snapshotSerializers": [
    "<rootDir>/node_modules/jest-serializer-vue"
  ]
},
```

Server-Side Rendering of Vue Components in Rails Products

Server-side rendering (SSR) is a technique to process the HTML first on your server before delivering it to client's browser to be displayed. Most of the time, SSR web pages are faster and have a lower time-to-content.

With faster web page and lower time-to-content, SSR web pages tend to have better user experience. On top of that, SSR content is search engine optimized (SEO)-friendly when compared to the client-side rendered web page. However there are also other concerns and constraints which you can read more at `https://ssr.vuejs.org/#what-is-server-side-rendering-ssr`

In this section, we will demonstrate a method to scaffold a server rendering component and possibly render a hello world using server rendering.

Scaffolding SSR Components in Rails Products

To generate a component with a SSR option, please run the following command:

```
rails vue:ssr
```

The `rails vue:ssr` command will generate a list of configurations and server-side rendering dependencies that can be found in the next section on manual configuration of server-side rendering.

You will need to scaffold a Rails view so that you can embed the SSR Vue component. In this case, we will generate "pages" via the scaffold generator:

```
rails generate scaffold pages
rails db:migrate
```

Let's embed the following code to the app/views/pages/index.html.erb:

```
<%= render_vue_component('VueComponent.js', :name => 'Hypernova The Renderer') %>
```

To run the Rails server first and follow by running node with the server-side rendering script:

```
rails server
node ssr
```

The finished text "Hello world" is server rendered as shown in Figure 4-4.

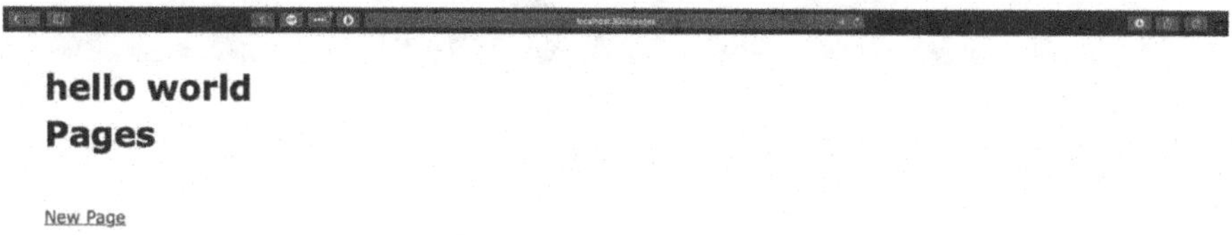

hello world
Pages

New Page

Figure 4-4. *Server-rendered "hello world" by the Hypernova gem*

You can generate further a server-side-rendered component with Vue generator followed by a `--ssr` option:

```
rails g vue <NAME> --ssr
```

The SSR component that will be generated by the `--ssr` option:

```
console.log("Hello, component")
const Vue = require("vue")
const renderVue = require("hypernova-vue").renderVue
const component = Vue.extend({
  template: '<h1>hello, component </h1>'
})
module.exports = renderVue("component.js", component)
```

If the name of the `render_vue` is wrong, a development warning like the one in Figure 4-5 will appear on the browser with an error `ReferenceError: Component "<name>" not registered`. Therefore, the name of the component at `ssr.js` should match that of the component at `app/javascripts/ssr/<name>.js`.

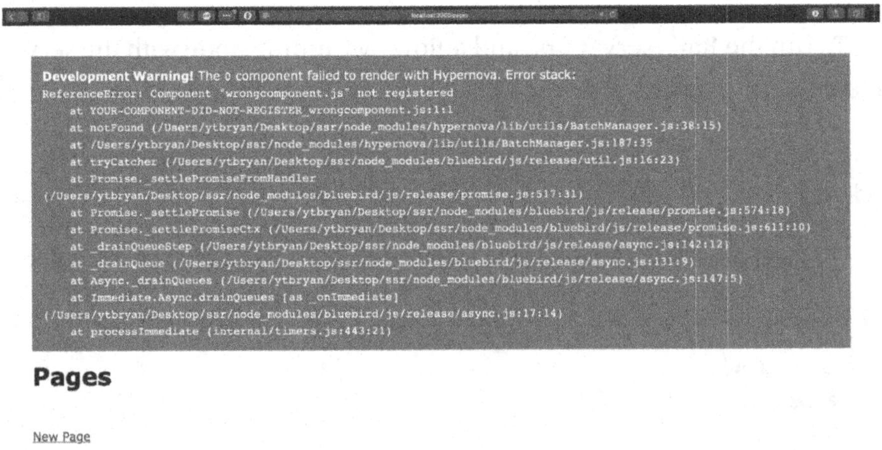

Figure 4-5. *A Rails view with ReferenceError: Component "wrongcomponent.js" not registered, produced by the Hypernova gem*

Manual Configuration of SSR Vue Components in Rails Products

This section introduces the configuration and manual changes required to enable SSR Vue components in Rails products. To get started with configuring server-side rendering manually, follow these steps:

1. Setup gem dependencies at Gemfile:

    ```
    gem 'hypernova'
    please run bundle
    ```

2. Install the npm dependencies:

    ```
    yarn add hypernova hypernova-vue vue-server-renderer
    ```

3. Add the following code to app/controllers/application_controller.rb:

    ```
    require 'hypernova'
    class ApplicationController < ActionController::Base
      around_action :hypernova_render_support
    end
    ```

4. Add the following code to app/helpers/application_helper.rb:

    ```
    require 'hypernova'

    module ApplicationHelper
      def ssr_vue(id, name)
        render_react_component(id, name: name)
      end
    end
    ```

5. Add the following code to config/initializer/
    hypernova.rb:

```
require 'hypernova'
require 'hypernova/plugins/development_mode_plugin'

Hypernova.add_plugin!(DevelopmentModePlugin.new)

Hypernova.configure do |config|
  config.host = "0.0.0.0"
  config.port = 7777            # The port where the
node service is listening
end
```

6. Add the following server.js to the root Rails
    project:

```
var hypernova = require('hypernova/server');

hypernova({
  devMode: true,
  getComponent(name) {
    console.log("The component name is -> " + name)
    if (name === 'VueComponent.js') {
      return require('./app/javascript/ssr/component.
js')
    }
    return null;
  },
  port: 7777,
});
```

7. Create a component.js file at app/javascript/ssr/
    component.js with the following code:

```
console.log("hello vue")
const Vue = require("vue")
const renderVue = require("hypernova-vue").renderVue

const MyComponentX = Vue.extend({
  template: '<h1>hello world</h1>'
})

module.exports = renderVue("VueComponent.js",
MyComponentX)
```

8. You will need a Rails view to embed your SSR Vue
    component. To generate a Rails view like pages, run
    rails generate scaffold pages at app/pages/
    index.html.erb:

```
<%= ssr_vue('VueComponent.js', :name => 'Hypernova
The Renderer') %>
```

Once you have manually edited all of the preceding configuration, you
should have server-side rendering in your Rails product.

Internationalization

Rails ship with a default internationalization library called i18n. It uses
the config/locales/en.yml file to translate languages into different
languages. In order to generate new languages, we create new .yml file as
shown in Figure 4-6.

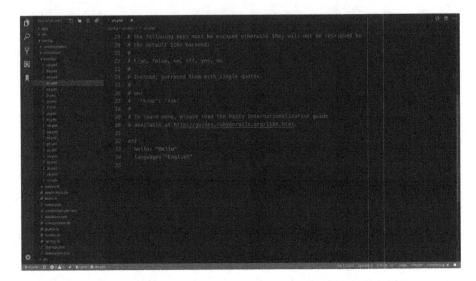

Figure 4-6. *The English YML locale file that resides in config/locales*

There are several internationalization packages in Vue community. The one that Vue on Rails ships by default is vue-i18n (`https://kazupon.github.io/vue-i18n/`), which is created and maintained by the Vue core team member, Kazuya Kawaguchi. By default, Vue on Rails extends vue-i18n to all its Vue components.

To point out the obvious difference, Rails' i18n uses .yml files, while Vue's vue-i18n uses .json files for internationalization purposes. Vue on Rails bridges the two i18n frameworks (Rails' i18n and Vue's vue-i18n) by converting one format to another in an amiable way. This makes it easy to reuse them within a Vue component.

To convert .yml files into .json files, simply run the rails vue:translate command at the root directory of the project.

This way, developers simply focus on building yml locales files within the app/config/locales directory since the json files will be based on a single source of truth (which is the yml files). This approach ensures minimal extra work required to make two i18n systems play nice with each other and keep themselves in sync.

Using Vue on Rails 118n

Let's get into action and try out Vue on the Rails' i18n example. We start by cloning the following repository:

```
git clone https://github.com/ytbryan/hello_robot.git
bundle
```

Once we have the cloned project and run bundle in it, we observe that all the Rails locale files reside in config/locales/*.yml locales for this example (see Figure 4-7).

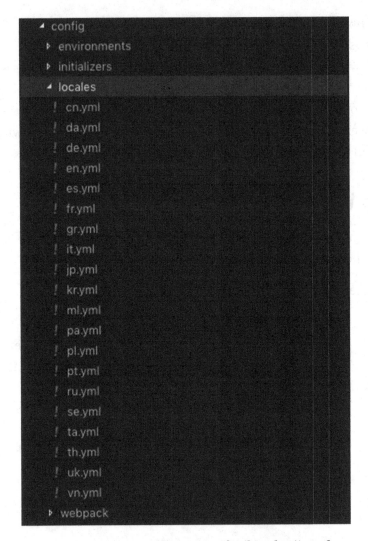

Figure 4-7. Rails' locales residing in config/locales/*.yml

Next, let's translate these .yml files into .json files so that Vue i18n can utilize them. We run `rails vue:translate` to generate the new json locales. You will observe the new json locales generated at app/ javascript/packs/locales/*.json (see Figure 4-8).

Figure 4-8. *Vue's locales residing in app/javascript/packs/locales/*.
json*

Next, let's make sure the npm dependencies are up to date and then
run the Rails server:

```
yarn install
rails server
```

Next we refresh the web page, and hello robot will be loaded with 20
locales of hellos (see Figure 4-9). This is because the yml locales are now
translated to json locales.

Hello Robot

"Bonjour" is hello in French

fr ▲▼

Figure 4-9. *The finished component of hello robot in French*

You can set up the internationalization support of Vue components in Rails products via the following command:

```
rails vue:i18n
```

Simple State Management of Vue Components Inside Rails Products

Sometimes, you would like your Vue component to remember the last timestamp or the last action of your users. It will be ideal if the Vue component can compute that automatically and store it efficiently among the components of the same page. This is where simple state management comes in handy. Vue ships with an official state management library, Vuex, which may be heavyweight for a simple component that requires simple state managing. Developer may prefer to adopt a simple state management that they may be able to roll up themselves. Let's explore simple state through an example repo.

Simple State Example

We will try to add a simple shared state among three components. Any changes to the shared state will be propagated to the other components. These changes do not require to communicate to the backend. All of these state changes are achieved without big tool like Vuex. Let's clone the simple state example from GitHub and update the dependencies.

```
git clone http://github.com/ytbryan/simple_state
bundle exec yarn install
bundle exec bundle install
```

Let's run the rails server to view a simple state example.

```
rails server
```

Try to click the buttons and observe how the shared state changes among the Vue components.

Figure 4-10 shows the example repo.

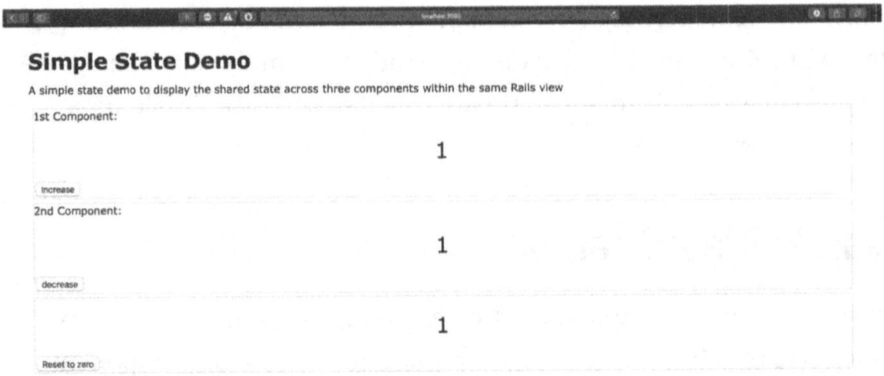

Simple State Demo

A simple state demo to display the shared state across three components within the same Rails view

1st Component:

1

Increase

2nd Component:

1

decrease

1

Reset to zero

Figure 4-10. *The finished component of a simple state example repo*

Scaffolding Simple State Management in Vue on Rails

The Vue on Rails gem ships with scaffolders and a simple store.js for state management. Sometimes, we want certain components to have shared state or we want to manually modify the store.js. To generate simple state support in Rails products, run the following command of Vue on Rails:

```
rails vue:store
```

To manually edit the store.js, use the following code and create a file at app/javascript/packs/store.js:

```
// Generated by Vue on Rails https://github.com/vueonrails/
vueonrails
// A simple state management as described in https://vuejs.org/
v2/guide/state-management.html

var store = {
  debug: true,
  state: {
```

```
    message: "Hello from Simple Store!"
  },
  setMessageAction(newValue) {
    if (this.debug) console.log("setMessageAction triggered
    with", newValue);
    this.state.message = newValue;
  },
  clearMessageAction() {
    if (this.debug) console.log("clearMessageAction
    triggered");
    this.state.message = "";
  }
};
```

```
export default store;
```

To generate a Vue component with simple state support, use the following command where <NAME> is the name of your V

```
rails g vue <NAME> --state
```

Wrap-up and the Next Step

And this concludes our short tutorial section of the book. Through these tutorials, we hope that you have learned how to setup the Vue on Rails project with configuration, create a nested Vue form, speed up your Vue on Rails product with server-side rendering, and even add simple state management to your Vue components and learned the internationalization of Vue components. To keep up to date with the latest features of Vue on Rails gem, you can follow the Vue on Rails GitHub repo at http://github.com/vueonrails/vueonrails. In the next chapter, we will dive into a more in-depth tutorial and show you how to build a real-time two-player game using Action Cable and Vue.

CHAPTER 5

Making a Real-Time Two-Player Game with Action Cable

A happy programmer is a productive programmer. That's why we optimize for happiness and you should too. Don't just pick tools and practices based on industry standards or performance metrics. Look at the intangibles: Is there passion, pride, and craftsmanship here? Would you truly be happy working in this environment eight hours a day?

—David Heinemeier Hansson

Action Cable was released in version 5 of Ruby on Rails and was one of the main features of this release. Most tutorials around Action Cable revolve around building a chat app, but here we are going to demonstrate another use – the two-player game. The underlying technology of Action Cable is Websockets, which is a tough concept to grasp at first for those who are used to the normal request and response flow of the HTTP protocol. In brief, Websockets are almost the opposite of HTTP requests; instead of the client making the request, the server sends data to the client or browser when it needs to. The client just needs to send one request to listen in on these events.

© Bryan Lim and Richard LaFranchi 2019
B. Lim and R. LaFranchi, *Vue on Rails*, https://doi.org/10.1007/978-1-4842-5116-4_5

In this tutorial for a two-player Tic Tac Toe game (see Figure 5-1), you'll realize that Action Cable is very easy to implement and in fact was the simplest part of building Tic Tac Toe. The tougher part was the design and ensuring game logic and rules are enforced properly, so this tutorial will be as much about software design as it is about Action Cable. Using Action Cable in a two-player game is important because you want to be able to broadcast updates from the server to the player's browser so that they can act when it is their turn. Action Cable allows us to do this without the need for polling the server or the need to refresh the page.

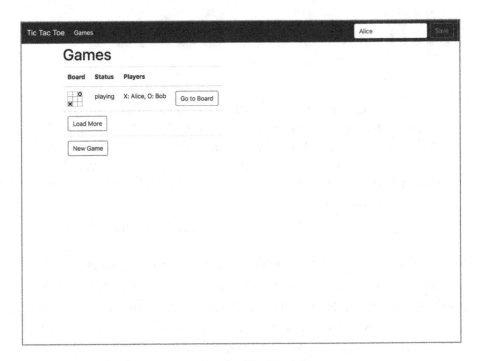

Figure 5-1. *The home page for the Tic Tac Toe app*

Note   The complete source code for the tutorial can be found at
`https://github.com/vueonrails/code-examples/tree/`
`master/tic_tac_toe` and full demo can be seen at `https://`
`vue-on-rails-tic-tac-toe.herokuapp.com`

Domain

The domain model consists of three models – Game, Player, and
GamesPlayer. GamesPlayer is a many-to-many association between Games
and Players. This basic design can be applied to all sorts of two-player
games with few modifications. The GamesPlayer model stores a piece
attribute (X or O), and we can define a couple validations to ensure there
will be at most two players who have joined a game.

```
validates_inclusion_of :piece, in: ['X', 'O']
validates_uniqueness_of :piece, scope: [:game, :player]
```

The Game model has a board attribute which stores the board serialized
as a JSON array of board pieces in the database (e.g., ["X", "O", "", "",
"", "", "", "", ""]). Along with the appropriate has_many associations,
the Game model also defines the following methods:

- x – A helper that returns the player who is currently
  joined as X

- o – A helper that returns the player who is currently
  joined as O

- status – Returns the status of the game:

  - waiting – Is returned until both players have joined
    the game

  - playing – Board is not filled and there is no winner

- over – Game is over and there is a winner

- tied – Returned when the board is full and there is no winner

- place(piece, position) – Method that validates whether or not a board placement is valid for the following conditions:

  - Position on the board is not already taken by another piece.

  - The piece being played is the correct turn (we assume that x always goes first).

  - The game is not already over or tied.

The GameChannel

In order to broadcast updates to a game, we can define an Action Cable channel, and the definition is the following.

```
class GameChannel < ApplicationCable::Channel
  def subscribed
    stream_from "game_channel_#{params[:game_id]}"
  end
end
```

The only parameter needed is the game_id, and we can define an after_commit hook to broadcast updates to a game. The game will be broadcasted to the players currently playing the game along with any onlookers who want to watch the action. ActionController provides a handy render function so that we can ensure consistency of the format broadcasted to the requests that are fetched.

```
class Game < Application Record
  after_commit :broadcast
  # ...

  private

  def broadcast
    game_json = GamesController.render 'games/show.json',
    assigns: { game: self }
    ActionCable.server.broadcast("game_channel_#{id}", game_
    json)
  end
end
```

The Controllers

The Game needs to support the following actions and we can provide those actions in a conventional manner for the most part. A Player is created for the session if it does not already exist, and we keep track of the current player by storing the player_id in the session.

- games#index – Lists games.

- games#create – Creates a Game.

- games#show – Shows the Game including its board.

- players#show – Gets the info for the current player (id, name).

- games_players#create – Joins a Game (as X or O).

- games_players#update – Player plays their turn.

One action that needs further discussing is the update action for
GamesPlayersController. We use this action to ensure that the current
player is the one requesting the update to prevent cheating and the proper
piece is placed in the position requested.

```ruby
# ex. put /games_players/123.json { position: 3 }
def update
 @games_player = current_player
.games_players
.find(params[:id])
  if @games_player.move(params[:position])
    render :show, status: :ok, location: @games_player
  else
    render json: { errors: @games_player.game.errors },
      status: :unprocessable_entity
  end
end
```

Note the move method that is being called, which in turn calls the place
method we described previously. This ensures that the correct piece will
be used to attempt to place in the board at the desired position and will
return false if any of the validations failed.

```ruby
def move(position)
  game.place(piece, position)
end
```

Now that we have discussed the basic design, it's time for the fun part
of using Vue to make game play interactive and real time. We will use the
Vuex Rails Plugin to manage state and define a Games, Game, and Board
components.

Listing Games

The only routes that need to support an html format are the games#index and games#show actions. The Games and Game components are initialized on these routes, respectively, and Turbolinks is used for navigation between the two. To ensure good performance, the JSON format for fetching games defaults to a limit of 10, and a "Load More" button is used for incrementing the limit by 10. Using the Vuex Rails Plugin allows us to do this in a simple manner. We won't go too deep into the html for the list, since it is just a simple table that lists a smaller version of the board, the game status, players, and a button link to view the game. Later we will discuss how to get real-time updates for the game list without a refresh. The complete code for the game list can be found under the directory app/javascript/parts/games/.

```
// app/javascript/parts/games/games.vue
<button
  class="btn btn-outline-dark"
  @click="loadMore()"
  :disabled="!anyMore">
  {{ anyMore ? 'Load More' : '...No More'}}
</button>
```

```
// app/javascript/parts/games/games.js
data: function() {
  return {
    limit: 10,
    anyMore: true
  }
},
created: function() {
  this.getGames()
},
```

```
methods: {
  // ...
  loadMore() {
    const currentCount = this.games.length
    this.limit += 10
    const vm = this
    this.getGames({limit: this.limit})
        .then(res => {
          const newCount = this.games.length
          if (newCount === currentCount) {
            vm.anyMore = false
          }
        })
        .catch(err => {
          console.error(err)
        })
    }
  }
```

Creating a Game

Creating a game doesn't require any fields, so it is just a simple button that calls the newGame() method, which performs the create action and redirects to the created game and board. We can use Turbolinks to perform this after we get the response and know the id of the created game.

```
<!- app/javascript/parts/games/games.vue -->
<button class="btn btn-outline-dark" @click="newGame()">New
Game</button>
```

```
// app/javascript/parts/games/games.js
methods: {
```

```
// ...
newGame() {
  this.createGame()
    .then(res => {
      Turbolinks.visit(`/games/${res.data.id}`)
    })
    .catch(err => { console.error(err) })
  }
}
```

Game Time

The game page simply shows two buttons, one for players to join as X and one for players to join as O and the interactive board. Also, depending on the state of the game, the buttons are disabled accordingly, so for example if two players have already joined a game, both buttons will be disabled to a third onlooker. Also, an alert shows when the game is completed and tells the players if they have won, lost, or tied. We also show some text to tell you whether you are playing the game.

```
// app/javascript/parts/game/game.vue
<template>
  <div class="row" v-if="game">
    <div class="col col-12 pb-2">
      <div class="d-flex justify-content-around">
        <button
          class="btn btn-outline-dark m-2"
          @click="join('X')"
          :disabled="isPlayingThisGame() ||
                  game.status != 'waiting'">
          {{ game.x ? (playingAs('X') ? 'You are' : game.x.name
          + ' is') + ' Playing' : 'Play'}} as X
```

```
        </button>
        <div class="alert alert-info" v-if="game.status ===
        'tied'">Tied Game</div>
        <div
          class="alert"
          :class="{'alert-success': game.winner.id ==
          currentPlayer.id,
                   'alert-danger': game.winner.id !=
                   currentPlayer.id}"
          v-if="game.winner && isPlayingThisGame()">
          {{ game.winner.id == currentPlayer.id ? 'You Win' :
          'You Lose' }}
        </div>
        <button
          class="btn btn-outline-dark m-2"
          @click="join('O')"
          :disabled="isPlayingThisGame() || game.status !=
          'waiting'">
          {{ game.o ? (playingAs('O') ? 'You are' : game.o.name
          + ' is') + ' Playing' : 'Play'}} as O
        </button>
      </div>
      <div class="d-flex justify-content-center">
        <board
          :game="game"
          :width="400"
          :myPiece="myPiece()">
        </board>
      </div>
    </div>
  </div>
</template>
```

Joining a Game

The buttons described previously call the join(piece) method, which simply uses the Vuex Rails plugin to call the create action on GamesPlayers. Once joined, a player may act if it is their turn.

```
join(piece) {
  const vm = this
  this.createGamesPlayer({game_id: this.game_id, piece: piece})
    .then(res => {
      vm.getGame(vm.game_id)
    })
    .catch(err => {
      alert(vm.error.errors)
    })
}
```

Drawing the Tic Tac Toe Board

The Board component is an SVG (created with the help of https://
vectr.com) which is essentially is a Tic Tac Toe board with all the Xs and
Os drawn in each position in the board (see Figure 5-2). We can then use
Vue to hide or show the correct pieces accordingly based on the state of
the game. vectr.com generates each element of the board with a unique
id, so these ids need to be mapped in correct order. In order to show a
lighter version of the pieces upon moussing over a particular position, we
also define invisible <rect> elements for each position towards the end
of the SVG. These elements will keep track of the current position and

handle click events when a player decides to place their X or O. The Board component also accepts a width prop and the full code lives under app/ javascript/parts/board/.

Figure 5-2. *SVG of Tic Tac Toe Board showing all elements*

The following code shows the template for the Tic Tac Toe board with all the Xs and Os and the appropriate SVG attributes to display the appropriate pieces based on the state of the game.

```
<!-- app/javascript/parts/board/board.vue -->
<template>
  <svg xmlns=http://www.w3.org/2000/svg
      xmlns:xlink="http://www.w3.org/1999/xlink
      version="1.1"
      preserveAspectRatio="xMidYMid meet"
      viewBox="0 0 600 600"
      :width="width"
      :height="width"
      @mouseleave="currentPosition = null"
      v-if="game && game.board">
    <def>
     <!- Unique element definitions with ids generated here ->
    </defs>
    <g>
      <!-- Squares for visibly showing the borders->
      <g v-for="(squareIds, position) in squareSvgIds">
        <use
          :xlink:href="squareIds[0]"
          opacity="1"
          fill="#ffffff"
          fill-opacity="1"/>
        <g :clip-path="'url(' + squareIds[1] + ')'">
          <use
            :xlink:href="squareIds[0]"
            opacity="1"
            fill-opacity="0"
            stroke="#000000"
            stroke-width="12"
            stroke-opacity="1" />
        </g>
      </g>
```

```
<!-- Os -->
<g v-for="(svgIds, position) in oSvgIds"
   v-if="game.board[position] === 'O' ||
         (game.board[position] === '' &&
         currentPosition === position &&
         myPiece === 'O')">
  <use
    :xlink:href="svgIds[0]"
    opacity="1"
    fill="#ffffff"
    fill-opacity="1" />
  <g :clip-path="'url(' + svgIds[1] + ')'">
    <use
      :xlink:href="svgIds[0]"
      opacity="1"
      fill-opacity="0"
      :stroke="game.board[position] === '' ? '#999999' :
      '#000000'"
      stroke-width="70"
      stroke-opacity="1" />
  </g>
</g>
<!-- Xs -->
<g v-for="(svgId, position) in xSvgIds"
   v-if="game.board[position] === 'X' ||
         (game.board[position] === '' &&
         currentPosition === position &&
         myPiece === 'X')">
  <use
    :xlink:href="svgId" opacity="1"
```

```
        :fill="game.board[position] === " ? '#999999' :
        '#000000'"
        fill-opacity="1" />
    </g>
    <!-- invisible elements to handle mouse enter events and
    click ->
    <template v-for="position in [0,1,2,3,4,5,6,7,8]">
      <rect
        :x="(position % 3) * 200"
        :y="position <= 2 ? 0 : (position <= 5 ? 200 : 400)"
        width="200"
      height="200"
      v-on:mouseenter="currentPosition = position"
      fill="transparent" @click="play(position)"/>
    </template>
  </g>
 </svg>
</template>
```

And of course in order to determine which piece to show, the Board component takes a myPiece prop, which can be X, O, or null. The null is necessary to ensure that any onlookers who aren't playing the game can't see or place any pieces when moving their mouse. Figure 5-3 shows how we show a lightened color of the player's piece while hovering over the appropriate position. We can set the color of the pieces using the fill="" attribute on the appropriate SVG element.

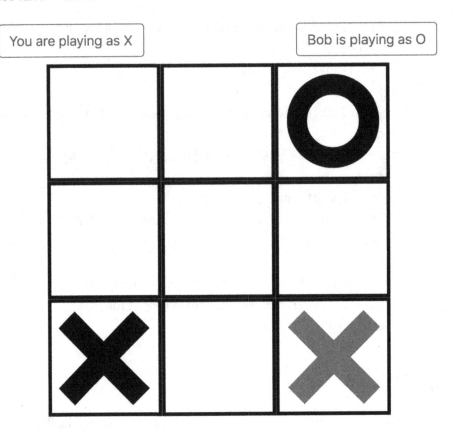

Figure 5-3. *Tic Tac Toe board with placed pieces and a position shown when moussing over, but not placed yet*

Placing a Piece

As we described early, placing a piece on the board calls the update action on GamesPlayers and in the preceding Board template we call the play(position) function on the appropriate <rect> element. The function calls the appropriate action and alerts any validations errors such as an out of turn move. You'll notice that the getGame() function is commented out. This is because we can subscribe to the GameChannel and will discuss this more in the next section.

```
play(position) {
  const vm = this
  if (this.game.board[position] != ") { return }
  const gp = this.game
   .games_players
   .find(gPlayer => gPlayer.piece === this.myPiece)
  this.updateGamesPlayer({
    id: gp.id,
    game_id: this.game.id,
    position: position
  })
  .then(res => {
    // this.getGame(vm.game.id)
  })
  .catch(err => {
    console.error(err)
    alert(vm.error ? vm.error.board : 'Something Went Wrong')
  })
}
```

Accessing Action Cable from Vue

As we mentioned in Chapter 3, we can easily create an Action Cable
consumer and define it as a prototype on Vue, which allows us to access
the consumer in any Vue instance or component. Be sure to add the
actioncable npm package – yarn add actionable.

```
// app/packs/hello_vue.js
import Vue from 'vue'
import ActionCable from 'actioncable'
Vue.prototype.$cable = ActionCable.createConsumer()
```

Subscribing to updates for a particular game is initialized in the created lifecycle hook and is really as simple as committing to the games/ UPDATE action provided by the Vuex Rails plugin.

```
// app/javascript/parts/game/game.js
created() {
  const vm = this
  this.channel = this.$cable.subscriptions.create({
    channel: 'GameChannel',
    game_id: this.game_id}, {
    received: function(data) {
      const item = JSON.parse(data)
      vm.$store.commit('games/UPDATE', { item })
    }
  })
}
```

Wait… Isn't there more? Nope, that is pretty much the gist of it. The subscription waits for any updates broadcasted by the server, and we parse the data when it is received and commit it to Vuex. Oh wait, there is one more step to ensure that we remove the subscription in the destroyed() lifecycle hook. This will ensure we unsubscribe from the channel when we don't need it anymore.

```
destroyed() {
  this.$cable.subscriptions.remove(this.channel)
}
```

Wrap-up and the Next Step

Besides some thought put into displaying the Game Board and ensuring players see the appropriate state for a Tic Tac Toe game, you can see how simple it is to use both normal HTTP requests and web socket subscriptions to keep backend state in sync with the browser. A lot of this is made possible if conventions are followed and data formats are consistent. Next, we will dive into Active Storage and how to build an interactive cropping tool for images.

CHAPTER 6

Building an Image-Cropping Tool with Vue and Active Storage

You want to enjoy life, don't you? If you get your job done quickly and your job is fun, that's good isn't it? That's the purpose of life, partly. Your life is better.

—Yukihiro Matsumoto

As developers, we often look to third-party libraries for solutions to problems that aren't easily solved or problems that we are not familiar with. This can be advantageous if we need to build a quick prototype, but there are downsides to this approach such as:

- Needing to rely on support for the library.

- Implementing with technologies such as Vue and Rails may not be straightforward.

B. Lim and R. LaFranchi, *Vue on Rails*, https://doi.org/10.1007/978-1-4842-5116-4_6

- Customization can sometimes be difficult.

- Bloat of a library may include unneeded/unwanted features or behavior.

Support is typically not an issue with libraries like Vue and Ruby on Rails because of the overwhelming community support, but it can be an issue with many JavaScript libraries. One feature common in web apps is an image-cropping tool, which there are certainly a few libraries out there that accomplish this. In this tutorial, we will roll our own image cropper using Vue and integrate it with direct uploads and the latest feature in Rails as of version 5.2 which is Active Storage. The biggest advantage of rolling your own is the learning experience, and that's what we will do in this chapter.

The Avatar

The avatar is one of the most common features in social media and other types of web applications. Often you would need to prepare a good image for yourself ahead of time because it is common for applications to automatically crop your avatar. This tutorial will show you how to build an interactive cropper with two basic goals in mind. It will accept any size image and allow you to pan and scale the image so that the area that is cropped is easily customized for the user.

It can be accomplished by supporting an original size uploaded image, allowing the user to pan the image to the appropriate location and a range slider to allow them to scale the image appropriately. Once these bounds are defined, the original image and bounds can be saved and processed as a variant as supported by Active Storage.

Active storage help and dependencies   This tutorial requires the web_processing ruby gem and activestorage npm package to be installed. More info and documentation about Active Storage can be found at https://edgeguides.rubyonrails.org/active_ storage_overview.html

The User Profile

The demo application will consist of a simple profile edit page shown at the edit action for Users (see Figure 6-1). An erb form will be used to demonstrate how we can build a Vue cropper component and embed the cropper within the form so the appropriate form fields are applied. The User model consists of three fields – name, avatar, and avatar_ crop. The avatar field will be the reference to the original size image, and avatar_crop is a string of the cropped geometry in the format of widthxheight+xoffset+yoffset which we will demonstrate how to generate this in the Vue cropper component and how to use the active storage variant helper to display it later in this chapter.

```
class User < ApplicationRecord
  has_one_attached :avatar
end
```

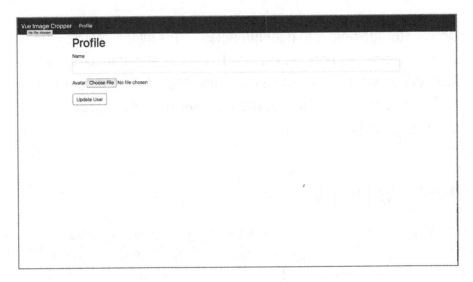

Figure 6-1. *The Edit Page for the User Profile*

The form for the user will use Rails helpers to demonstrate how we can continue to use erb and spice things up a bit with some fancy Vue components. Inside the form is an element with a cropper id which we will mount the cropper Vue component to. Another important field to note is the active storage field helper, which is a file field with `direct_upload: true` option. All this option does is add a `data-direct-upload-url` attribute to the field so we know where to submit the image file.

```
<h1>Profile</h1>
<%= form_for @user do |f| %>
  <div class="form-group">
    <%= f.label :name %>
    <%= f.text_field :name, class: 'form-control' %>
  </div>
  <div class="form-group">
    <%= f.label :avatar %>
    <%= f.file_field :avatar, direct_upload: true, accept:
    "image/*" %>
```

```
    <div id="cropper"></div>
  </div>
  <%= f.submit class: 'btn btn-outline-dark' %>
<% end %>
```

Direct uploads   Direct uploads is a feature supported by Active
Storage that allows you to save some server resources by having
image and file uploads go directly from a user's browser to a cloud
object storage service such as Amazon S3.

Vue Cropper Component

The cropper component will use the DirectUpload module provided by
the activestorage npm package to upload the image directly when a file is
added to the input. Just like we used SVG in the Tic Tac Toe tutorial, we will
also use an SVG to display a simple square that shows the area of the image
to be cropped along with a few elements to show some padding with some
slight transparency. <rect> SVG elements are a simple way to display such
shapes and note that they take x,y,width, and height attributes where x and
y are offsets from the top-left corner of an SVG. The SVG will be a square
400 x 400 with the cropped area being 300 x 300 with an x and y offset of 50
to center the cropped area (see Figure 6-2).

Figure 6-2. *Bunny Cropper (Photo source: Pixabay, used under the Pixabay License[1])*

The dimensions are defined as data attributes on the component but will remain static for the purposes of this demo. In theory, it could also support resizing the cropping area, but that is outside the scope of this tutorial. It is important to note the data attributes defined on the component as seen in the following code and found in app/javascript/parts/cropper/cropper.js.

```
data: function() {
  return {
    directUploadUrl: null, // url used in direct uploads
```

---

[1]License: https://pixabay.com/service/license/. Image: https://pixabay.com/photos/bunny-rabbit-easter-pet-animal-1149060/

```
    fileField: null, // the original active storage file input
    file: null, // the file object loaded
    blobSrc: null, // the image data for displaying the image
    blobSignedId: null, // id returned from direct upload
    name: null, // User's Name
    x: 50, // x offset for cropping area
    y: 50, // y offset for cropping area
    width: 300, // width of the cropping area
    height: 300, // height of the cropping area
    image_width: null, // actual width of the loaded image
    image_height: null, // actual height of the loaded image
    image_x: 0, // x offset of the image updated on panning
    image_y: 0, // y offset of the image updated on panning
    scale: 1, // image scale - adjusted to fit when loaded
    dragging: false // true when actively panning
  }
}
```

The complete Vue Cropper template found in app/javascript/parts/ cropper/cropper.vue is shown in the following code. We will go into more detail about each element in this chapter and how we use Vue to make the elements interactive.

```
<template>
  <div id="cropper" v-if="blobSrc && image_width && image_
height">
    <div class="form-group">
      <label for="imageScale">Image Scale</label>
      <input
        type="range"
        min="10"
        max="100"
```

```
      v-model="imageScale"
      name="imageScale"
      id="imageScale">
    <p class="text-muted">{{ this.imageScale }}% size of
    original image</p>
  </div>

  <div class="dropper">
    <svg
      width="400"
      height="400"
      @mousemove="pan($event)"
      @scroll="zoomImage($event)">
      <image
        :xlink:href="blobSrc"
        :x="image_x"
        :y="image_y"
        :width="scaledWidth"
        :height="scaledHeight">
      </image>

      <!-- BEGIN elements for showing darker background
      outside cropped area -->
      <rect
        x="0"
        y="0"
        :width="x"
        height="400"
        fill="#000000"
        fill-opacity="0.5"/>
      <rect
        :x="x"
```

```
        y="0"
        :width="width"
        :height="y"
        fill="#000000" fill-opacity="0.5"/>
    <rect
        :x="x"
        :y="y + height"
        :width="width"
        :height="400 - y - height"
        fill="#000000"
        fill-opacity="0.5"/>
    <rect
        :x="x + width"
        y="0"
        :width="400 - x - width"
        height="400"
        fill="#000000"
        fill-opacity="0.5"/>
    <!-- END -->

    <!-- allows panning image -->
    <rect
        :x="x"
        :y="y"
        :width="width"
        :height="height"
        fill="#FFFFFF"
        fill-opacity="0"
        :class="dragging ? 'grabbing' : 'grab'"
        @mousemove="pan($event)"
        @mousedown="dragging = true"
        @mouseup="dragging = false"
```

```
        @mouseleave="dragging = false"/>
    </svg>
</div>

<!-- hidden fields to reference direct upload image and
area to crop-->
<input type="hidden" name="user[avatar]"
:value="blobSignedId">
<input type="hidden" name="user[avatar_crop]"
:value="croppedGeometry">

  </div>
</template>
```

Loading the Image

In the mounted() lifecycle hook of the Cropper component, we search for
the avatar file input and listen for changes. When a file is added, we call
the fileAdded() function defined in methods in the component as seen in
the following code. The function first grabs the file from the event, creates
a new upload using the DirectUpload module, loads the image source, sets
the image height and width, sets the scale of the image to fit the SVG size,
sets the blobSrc attribute to the data of the image, sets the blobSignedId
to that of the response of the direct upload, and then removes the input
field. Once a file is loaded, we see the cropping tool along with a range
slider for scaling the image as seen in Figure 6-3.

77% size of original image

Figure 6-3. The Range Slider for scaling images

```
// looking for the file input field when the component is
mounted
mounted: function() {
  this.fileField = document.querySelector('input[type="file"]')
  this.directUploadUrl = this.fileField.dataset.directUploadUrl
  this.name = this.fileField.name
  this.fileField.onchange = this.fileAdded
}

// Method called when file is loaded into the input.
fileAdded(event) {
  const vm = this
  this.file = event.target.files[0]
  if (this.file) {
    const upload = new DirectUpload(this.file, this.
    directUploadUrl)
    upload.create((error, blob) => {
      if (error) {
        console.error(error)
        alert(error.toString())
      } else {
        console.debug(blob)
        const image = new Image()
        image.onload = function() {
          vm.image_width = image.width
          vm.image_height = image.height
          if (vm.image_height > 400) {
            vm.scale = 400 / vm.image_height
          }
        }
        image.src = URL.createObjectURL(this.file)
        vm.blobSrc = image.src
```

```
        vm.blobSignedId = blob.signed_id
        vm.fileField.value = null
        vm.fileField.name = null
        vm.fileField.remove()
      }
    })
  }
}
```

Panning the Image

Panning the image requires a bit of CSS to show the grab and grabbing cursor along with a few mouse events. We set the dragging attribute to true on @mousedown and set it to false on @mouseup or @mouseleave. The @mouseleave event is necessary so that there isn't unexpected behavior if the mouse is held and moved outside the cropping area. The @mousemove event calls the pan() function and simply updates the image_x and image_y fields based on the movement of the mouse as seen in in the following code.

```
<!-- The cropping area SVG element that supports panning -->
<rect
  :x="x"
  :y="y"
  :width="width"
  :height="height"
  fill="#FFFFFF"
  fill-opacity="0"
  :class="dragging ? 'grabbing' : 'grab'"
  @mousemove="pan($event)"
  @mousedown="dragging = true"
```

```
@mouseup="dragging = false"
@mouseleave="dragging = false"/>
```

The pan() method simply updates the x and y attributes for the image as shown in the following code.

```
// app/javascript/parts/cropper.js
pan(evt) {
  if (this.dragging) {
    this.image_x += evt.movementX
    this.image_y += evt.movementY
  }
}
```

Scaling the Image

When the image is loaded into the Cropper, we scaled it down if needed to fit the bounds of the 400 x 400 SVG. We also allow the tool to change the scale of the image using a range slider. The slider is based on percentage of the original size of the image, so we define a computed property to convert the scale attribute percentage to decimal and vice versa. The scale attribute is then used to show the correct size of the image in view. When the slider is moved back and forth, the image is then scaled appropriately. Figure 6-4 illustrates image scaling.

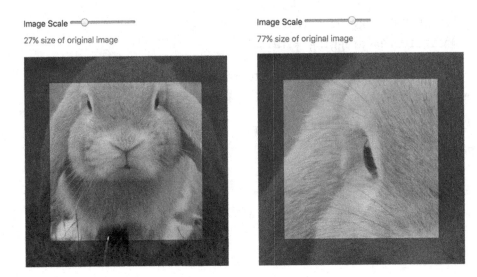

Figure 6-4. *Demonstration of scaling an image (Photo source: Pixabay)*

The input field for the range slider and the computed property are shown in the following code:

```
<input
  type="range"
  min="10"
  max="100"
  v-model="imageScale"
  name="imageScale"
  id="imageScale">
```

```
// app/javascript/parts/cropper.js
imageScale: {
  get: function() {
    return parseInt(this.scale * 100)
  },
```

```
  set: function(newVal, oldVal) {
    this.scale = newVal / 100
  }
}
```

ImageMagick Processing

We mentioned earlier that we would use the avatar_crop attribute to store the image geometry we want to use. To get it in the correct format, we can define it as a computed property and bind it to a value on a hidden input field. When the form is submitted, the dimensions are saved, and we can apply the geometry as a variant when displaying the avatar. The computed method, input field, and avatar link can be seen in the following code.

The croppedGeometry() computed property returns a string in the proper format used by ImageMagick.

```
croppedGeometry: function() {
  const scaledWidth = parseInt(this.width / this.scale)
  const scaledHeight = parseInt(this.height / this.scale)
  const scaledXOffset = this.x - parseInt(this.image_x / this.
  scale)
  const scaledYOffset = this.y - parseInt(this.image_y / this.
  scale)
  return `${scaledWidth}x${scaledHeight}+${scaledXOffset}+${sca
  ledYOffset}`
}
```

Next, we see the hidden input field for the image geometry which binds the previous computed property to its value attribute.

```
<input
  type="hidden"
  name="user[avatar_crop]"
  :value="croppedGeometry">
```

Finally, we can display the avatar at various sizes using the saved geometry. An example is shown in Figure 6-5.

```
<%= image_tag(@user.avatar.variant(crop: @user.avatar_crop,
resize: '100x100')) %>
```

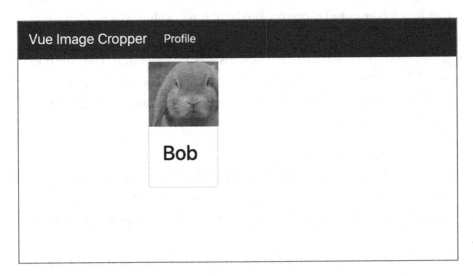

Figure 6-5. *Displaying a thumbnail of the upload profile picture (Photo source: Pixabay)*

And that concludes the image-cropping tutorial. We can see how to achieve a very effective cropping tool with very little effort and avoid the frontend development emergency off ramp, and it was a lot of fun in the process.

Wrap-up and the Next Step

That concludes our hands-on part of the book. We find it best to learn by example and hope that these tutorials provided a lot of insight into what can be accomplished with Vue and Ruby on Rails. In the next chapter, we shift our gears to turbo mode for your Vue on Rails project with deployment, testing, and troubleshooting without losing your mind.

PART III

Turbo Charge – Production Ready

Chapter 7. Testing, Deployment, and Troubleshooting

Chapter 8. Conclusion – Finishing the Race

CHAPTER 7

Testing, Deployment, and Troubleshooting

This chapter contains three small chapters in one, namely, Testing, Deployment, and Troubleshooting. They do not aim to be complete guides for these topics but to provide the essentials for those who are starting this journey and how they apply to a Vue on Rails approach.

Testing Approaches

The software testing world is a whole discipline in itself apart from the development world. Large companies have dedicated QA/QC departments to offload the burden from engineers. The theory is that engineers spend the time doing what they do best – engineering. But what if you work on a small team or project? What if you are a one-human shop? You'll have to make some tradeoffs depending on the type of project you are working on and the consequences that could happen if a severe bug is introduced. Could one of your customers lose money? Is sensitive information at risk if the project is hacked? Is it a software system that could potentially cause human injury? Or even worse – death?

There are tradeoffs for everything, but the main goal in software testing is to catch bugs before they are released, and the best way to do this is to maintain a suite of regression tests so that bugs aren't introduced after

© Bryan Lim and Richard LaFranchi 2019
B. Lim and R. LaFranchi, *Vue on Rails*, https://doi.org/10.1007/978-1-4842-5116-4_7

implementing a new feature. We'll talk about how to do that in a Vue on Rails approach with the idea of keeping it simple and will be geared towards low-consequence projects where your small team may or may not have the time and money to spend on testing. If you work on a high-consequence project, make sure you have the budget for a proper QA/QC cycle before releasing. That being said, a low-consequence project doesn't mean you have to produce a low-quality product. There is a good balance between development and testing that aligns with the Vue on Rails approach of keeping things with Vue's simplicity and the conventions of Rails.

TDD – To Drive or Not to Drive?

TDD or test-driven development is a development process that encourages writing tests first before writing the actual code for the software. The idea is to write a test for a feature or a test that reproduces an existing bug in the software, make sure the test fails as expected, then write the code that makes the test pass, and finally refactor code if necessary and make sure the test still passes.

In my experience I have seen many developers and product managers argue about the benefits of TDD. First, stop arguing about it. Every developer and team is different, some do strictly TDD, some do it on occasion, and some not at all. We'll leave that decision up to your team. I find TDD to be useful in scenarios that are not very straightforward and a solution is not easily attained. The test first approach could help jumpstart the problem-solving process in certain scenarios. TDD is often considered as a way to drive correctness of code from developers' perspective.

What about RSpec and BDD?

An extension of TDD called behavior-driven development or BDD is a different way of looking at testing from a user's or stakeholder's perspective and created in a way that all parties involved in a project can understand. RSpec is a testing framework inspired by BDD that is widely adopted in the Ruby on Rails community. BDD and the decision to use RSpec should up to your team as well. If Rails testing that is supported out of the box is sufficient for the project, then there is not much need to use RSpec.

General Testing Guidelines

Regardless of the testing styles you choose to adopt, here is a list of general guidelines that we recommend for testing:

- Unit test methods that aren't trivial in the business model.

- Write at least one integration test for get actions show/index.

- Write two tests for create/update actions. One for success/and one that fails on validation errors also known as the *happy path* vs. *dark path.*

- Write system tests/e2e tests for core features.

- If bugs occur, write a test integration/or unit to reproduce it and fix the bug.

- System tests will catch a lot of bugs on the Vue side, but it may also help to write unit tests for Vue components.

- UI/browser tests can be fragile so don't overdo it. More time will be spent fixing fragile tests than actual development.

System Tests

System tests are important in environments that integrate Vue and Rails because it provides an end-to-end solution to testing the integration of the two technologies. The latest version of Rails supports system tests out of the box. System tests are essentially a wrapper around Capybara for writing clean and simple tests that interact directly with the browser using helper methods such as `click_on`, `fill_in`, and `assert_selector`. Before system tests were integrated into the Rails framework, configuration was necessary for this to work, and JavaScript was not supported out of the box.

We will demonstrate an example for testing our two-player Tic Tac Toe game that we built in Chapter 5. This is a unique situation because we'll need to have multiple browser sessions to be able to test a game from start to end. Luckily Capybara has a `use_session` method just for this purpose. The test starts a new game in the main browser session and joins as X. In the other session, the other player joins the game created and plays as O. A series of pieces are placed and we swap between sessions and play until the game is over.

```ruby
require "application_system_test_case"

class MultiSessionsTest < ApplicationSystemTestCase
  test "visiting the index" do
    visit root_path
    click_on "New Game"
    click_on "Play as X"
    assert_text "You are Playing as X"

    Capybara.using_session :o do
      visit root_path
      click_on "Go to Board", match: :first
      click_on "Play as O"
      assert_text "You are Playing as O"
    end
```

```
x_positions = [0, 4, 8]
o_positions = [1, 3]

while x_positions.length > 0
  x_pos = x_positions.shift
  play(x_pos)
  assert_piece(x_pos, :X)

  if o_positions.length > 0
    o_pos = o_positions.shift
    Capybara.using_session :o do
      assert_piece(x_pos, :X)
      play(o_pos)
      assert_piece(o_pos, :O)
    end
    assert_piece(o_pos, :O)
  end
end

assert_text "You Win"

Capybara.using_session :o do
  assert_text "You Lose"
end

  end
end
```

So, the preceding code covers a happy path of a game from start
to end with one winner and one loser. We've defined a couple helper
methods – play and assert_piece. The play method clicks on the
appropriate board position and assert_piece checks that the appropriate
piece has been played. For this to work, we also need to define an id
attribute on the related SVG element such as "X5" denoting that an X is

visible in the fifth board index. Helper methods can be defined in the `ApplicationSystemTestCase` class since all our test cases for system tests extend from that class.

What about other scenarios such as a tied game? Or a different board configuration? We could create a few helper methods to cover these scenarios in a system test, but it is not the best approach. Each system test adds a bit of overhead to the time it takes to run your test suite. These scenarios would be better covered in a typical Rails unit test. If there is a UI scenario that needs to be covered, we could also use Jest and Vue test utilities to create a unit for a particular Vue component. This leads us into the discussion of such testing tools and frameworks that we can use for unit testing Vue components.

Vue Test Utilities and Jest

When unit testing Vue components, it is easy to get carried away with testing lots of edge cases just like it can be with system tests. So, it is important to think about the important pieces of a component. Take the Board component in the Tic Tac Toe game, for example. It would be unrealistic to test every possible board configuration, and we aren't necessarily even interested in that since a game object is passed down as a prop. The important part of the component is testing that when a player clicks on a certain board position, it results in the appropriate action being called; in this case, it is the Vuex action for `games_players/UPDATE`. The vue-test-utils documentation has some good examples on testing Vuex action, so we will follow those guidelines for testing this scenario.

Documentation   Vue test utilities and Jest have great documentation and can be found respectively at `https://vue-test-utils.vuejs.org` and `https://jestjs.io`

Generating a Vue Unit Test

The vuejs gem includes the option to generate a test when you generate a component. The following commands will check if Vue testing is setup for your Rails project and generate a component that includes a test file.

```
rails vue:test
rails generate vue something --test
```

This will generate a scaffold of a very simple test along with the component that is generated. The test is generated at the path app/javascript/test/something.test.js. The following test code is generated.

```
import { shallowMount } from '@vue/test-utils'
import App from '@/some.vue'

describe('some.vue', () => {
  it('render hello some', () => {
    const message = "Hello some!"
    const wrapper = shallowMount(App)
    expect(wrapper.find('#some').text()).toBe(message)
  })
})
```

To run all your *.test.js files that live in app/javascript/, simply run the following command:

```
yarn test
```

This runs any test that matches the *.test.js pattern with app/javascript.

Testing the Tic Tac Toe Board Component

The following example uses the Jest mockImplementation() method, which returns a promise. We can create a few unit tests that cover the following:

- A simple test that ensures an SVG element is rendered

- A test that ensures the games_players/update Vuex action is called for an empty board position

- A test for checking that the games_player/update Vuex action is not called when a position has already been played

A lot of examples take advantage of the great documentation about testing Vuex in the official vue-test-utils documentation. The examples trigger the position click action by finding the first <rect> element in the Board component.

```
import { shallowMount, createLocalVue } from '@vue/test-utils'
import Board from './board.vue'
import Vuex from 'vuex'
const localVue = createLocalVue()
localVue.use(Vuex)

describe('Board', () => {
  let actions
  let store

  beforeEach(() => {
    actions = {
      update: jest.fn().mockImplementation(cb => cb)
    }
```

```
    store = new Vuex.Store({
      state: {},
      modules: {
        games_players: {
          namespaced: true,
          state: {
            all: [],
            current: null,
            error: null
          },
          actions
        }
      }
    })
  })

test('renders an svg', () => {
  const wrapper = shallowMount(Board, { store, localVue })
  expect(wrapper.contains('svg'))
})

test('calls games_players update action', () => {
  const wrapper = shallowMount(Board, { store, localVue })
  wrapper.setProps({
    myPiece: 'X',
    width: 400,
    game: {
      id: 1,
      board: ['','O','X','','','','','',''],
      games_players: [
        {
          id: 1,
          game_id: 1,
```

```
                player_id: 1,
                piece: 'X'
              },
              {
                id: 2,
                game_id: 1,
                player_id: 2,
                piece: 'O'
              }
            ]
          }
        })
      wrapper.find('rect').trigger('click')
      expect(actions.update).toHaveBeenCalled()
    })

    test('does not call games_players update action for existing
  piece', () => {
        const wrapper = shallowMount(Board, { store, localVue })
        wrapper.setProps({
          myPiece: 'X',
          width: 400,
          game: {
            id: 1,
            board: ['X','O',",",",",",",","],
            games_players: [
              {
                id: 1,
                game_id: 1,
                player_id: 1,
                piece: 'X'
              },
```

```
      {
        id: 2,
        game_id: 1,
        player_id: 2,
        piece: 'O'
      }
    ]
  }
})
wrapper.find('rect').trigger('click')
expect(actions.update).not.toHaveBeenCalled()
})
})
```

Heroku – The Ninja Deployment

This simple command has been a developer's dream come true.

```
git push heroku master
```

For most small- to medium-sized projects, we recommend Heroku as a platform for publishing applications, especially if you don't have the resources for a dedicated DevOps team or system admin. The Ninja command covers the basics, and Heroku now supports Webpacker and will build our necessary Vue component assets along with any assets handled by sprockets. You'll still need to think about how to handle migrations and will need to think about Redis addons to support background jobs and Action Cable if needed by your application.

Heroku vs. Virtual Private Server

There are plenty of cloud providers that offer virtual private servers (VPS) such as Digital Ocean, Amazon Web Services, Google Cloud, and many other providers. A VPS is a server that runs in a virtual environment on shared physical hardware. Hardware is maintained by the cloud provider, so swapping out bad disks, CPUs, etc. VPS providers often give you the choice of which operating system you would like to run with different flavors of Linux such as CentOS or Ubuntu. This may be a viable option for developers who also like to get into the nitty gritty of system administration or have more resources to support maintenance and monitoring of the servers. Be sure to weigh in on all the tradeoffs of this approach. We have listed the advantages and disadvantages of each option for you to evaluate.

Heroku advantages:

- Ninja deployment in one command

- Third-party addon support such as Redis support

- Automated SSL certificates for hobby level

- No time consumed by system monitoring and administration

Heroku disadvantages:

- Expensive for large-scale projects (some may argue that cost is offset by not needing some large ops team)

- Less control over the environment

VPS advantages:

- More control of the environment. So control over networking and firewalls if you need a private environment.

- Inexpensive (as little as $5/month for basic VPS).

- Learning how to setup NGINX/Apache along with a production Ruby environment using Passenger or Unicorn is a good learning experience and a very valuable skill.

- Learning how to setup and administer a database such as Postgres or MySQL is also a valuable skill.

VPS disadvantages:

- Setting up a Rails-ready production environment takes time.

- Deployments can be automated using tools such as Capistrano, but configuring Capistrano is often non-trivial.

- Overhead of maintaining and monitoring a server such as monitoring memory, CPU, and disk usage. Some cloud providers offer automatic scaling, but other service providers may not.

Continuous Integration and Deployment

Whether we are using Heroku or a VPS, we can take advantage of various continuous integration services such as Travis CI to combine and automate our test, build, and deploy process. This will come in handy especially if we want our application to support different browsers. If you are developing in Chrome on a Mac, how do you know if our Vue components are supported on Firefox on a PC? A great service for this is BrowserStack and provides the ability to test various browsers on multiple operating systems. We can ensure our testing phase passes before the application is deployed to production. Also, if we need a finer grained release management, then we can choose only to deploy when a release is tagged in our git repo or under other conditions. We will demonstrate how to set up Travis CI to include a custom test and deploy process which integrates with BrowserStack and Heroku. To get started you'll want to sign up for accounts at travis-ci.org and browserstack.com.

Travis CI

Travis CI is a popular continuous integration tool that easily integrates with GitHub and other tools such as BrowserStack. Travis CI has some great documentation on getting started, so we won't go into too much detail, but will show a `.travis.yml` configuration file which we can use to perform the following CI process in three stages:

- Testing stage which runs our unit and integration tests including our Vue unit tests

- A staging deployment phase which gets our latest code up to our Heroku staging environment

- A BrowserStack phase which runs our system tests against our Heroku staging URL

The following is an example Travis CI yaml configuration file.

```
language: ruby
rvm:
- 2.5.5
cache:
  - bundler
  - yarn
env:
  secure: # use travis encrypt
before_script: bin/yarn
jobs:
  include:
  - stage: test
```

```
      name: Rails Unit/Integration Tests
      script: bin/rails test
    - name: Jest Unit Tests
      script: bin/yarn test
    - stage: deploy staging
      deploy:
         provider: heroku
         app: vueonrails-ci-staging
         run: bin/rails db:migrate
         strategy: git
         api_key:
            secure: # … use travis encrypt
    - stage: test staging
      name: firefox
      script: TASK_ID=0 bin/rails test:system
    - name: chrome
      script: TASK_ID=1 bin/rails test:system
    - name: safari
      script: TASK_ID=2 bin/rails test:system
    - name: internet explorer
      script: TASK_ID=3 bin/rails test:system
```

This configuration allows us to perform multiple tasks in parallel within the three stages we mentioned. Running our Rails unit and integration tests along with the Heroku deployment are straightforward as long as we encrypt and add our api key for Heroku using the travis encrypt command. Using BrowserStack to run our system tests against multiple browsers is not as trivial. This stage is broken up into four tasks, one for each browser. Next, we'll discuss how to configure BrowserStack to work properly.

BrowserStack

BrowserStack has the capability to run its tests against our local test server, but ideally, we want to run the tests against our staging environment on Heroku to test an environment as close as possible to production. System tests use Capybara under the hood, so we can simply set our app host for Capybara in our `test/test_helper.rb` file.

```
Capybara.app_host = 'https://staging-app.herokuapp.com:443'
```

You'll notice that our Travis CI configuration for the BrowserStack stage includes a TASK_ID variable in the command. Our code for setting up BrowserStack uses this value to determine which browser to run against. We can define a `config/browserstack.yml` file which includes this configuration.

```
server: "hub-cloud.browserstack.com"
common_caps:
  "browserstack.debug": true
browser_caps:
  -
    browser: firefox
  -
    browser: chrome
  -
    browser: safari
  -
    browser: internet explorer
```

We can now setup a custom Capybara driver that uses the TASK_ID to select the appropriate browser to run against.

```
TASK_ID = (ENV['TASK_ID'] || 0).to_i
```

```
CONFIG = YAML.load(File.read(Rails.root.join("config",
"browserstack.yml")))
CONFIG['user'] = ENV['BROWSERSTACK_USERNAME'] || CONFIG['user']
CONFIG['key'] = ENV['BROWSERSTACK_ACCESS_KEY'] || CONFIG['key']

Capybara.register_driver :browserstack do |app|
  Capybara.app_host = 'https://vueonrails-ci-staging.herokuapp.
  com:443'
  @caps = CONFIG['common_caps'].merge(CONFIG['browser_caps']
  [TASK_ID])

  Capybara::Selenium::Driver.new(app,
    :browser => :remote,
    :url => "http://#{CONFIG['user']}:#{CONFIG['key']}@#{CONFIG
    ['server']}/wd/hub",
    :desired_capabilities => @caps
  )
end
```

You'll notice that the code uses BROWSERSTACK_USERNAME and BROWSERSTACK_ACCESS_KEY environment variables. We can encrypt these values to include in our travis config file using the travis cli, for example.

```
travis encrypt BROWSERSTACK_USERNAME=...
```

Finally, we just need to update our test/application_system_test_case.rb to inform Rails to use the Browserstack server by using the driven_by method.

```
class ApplicationSystemTestCase <
ActionDispatch::SystemTestCase
  driven_by :browserstack
end
```

And that about wraps things up for using Travis CI to automate a lot of tasks that we often see in development environment that moves a quick pace and quick iterations. Let's see how our tests performed in the Travis CI dashboard (see Figure 7-1)

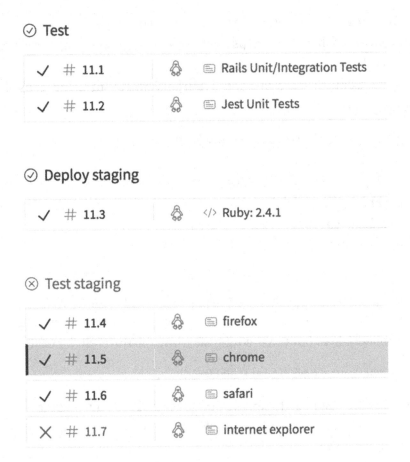

Figure 7-1. Travis CI results dashboard

DOH! ... always causing problems IE. Good thing we didn't deploy it to production. Note that our Travis CI configuration doesn't include a deployment process to production, but this can be easily done by adding another deployment stage once all previous stages have completed in a similar manner to our staging deployment. Following a good process for getting your app into production isn't always clear especially for small development teams that also need to do their own DevOps, so we wanted to make the testing and deployment phase of a project straightforward and hope you appreciate our approach which aligns with our philosophy of simplicity.

Troubleshooting Common Issues of Vue on Rails

In this section, we explore some common and sometimes thorny issues of Vue on Rails projects that you may stumble upon. If you need further help, you could list it on stackoverflow.com as Vue on Rails or you could always list an issue at the Webpacker project (`http://github.com/rails/Webpacker`). Each of the following issues is covered in this section.

1. In a Vue on Rails project with Webpacker, can I import the Vue on Rails project into Vue UI?

2. In a Vue on Rails project with Webpacker, how do I change the compile path from app/javascript/packs to something else?

3. In a Vue on Rails project with Webpacker, how do I use embedded Ruby (Erb) inside your Webpacker project?

4. How do I fix the error "Cannot find module <name_of_module>"?

5. How do I solve an error that says "TypeError: undefined is not an object (evaluating 'options.components')"?

6. In a Vue on Rails project with Webpacker, how do I disable fingerprinting to create Vue.js widget component?

7.   How do I solve the following Vue error: "Did you register the component correctly? For recursive components, make sure to provide the name option."

8.   Is there a way to use npm instead of yarn as the default package manager?

9.   For Vue on Rails project with Webpacker, how do I manage Node and Rails environments?

10. For Vue on Rails projects with Webpacker, is there a way to bypass the IE 11 issues on Windows?

11. For Vue on Rails projects with Webpacker, shouldn't package X be in the dependencies instead of devDependencies?

12. How do I solve this Heroku error: "No default language could be detected for this app"?

13. How do I solve this Heroku error: "App not compatible with buildpack"?

This chapter assumes your Vue on Rails uses Webpacker as the default Webpack manager.

1. In a Vue on Rails project with Webpacker, can I import the Vue on Rails project into Vue UI?

Vue UI is a web application that you can run to manage Vue projects and is a feature of vue-cli. To make Vue on Rails compatible with Vue UI, you will need to add the @vue/cli-service package into devdependencies of package.json:

```
yarn add @vue/cli-service --dev
```

With the Vue UI installed, you can import the Vue on Rails project by clicking Import > Go to the Vue on Rails project and click Import this project.

2. In a Vue on Rails project with Webpacker, how do I change the compile path from app/javascript/packs to something else?

You may wish to use a different directory to store your Vue components or javascript. You can change the directory name or the path at Webpacker.yml.

3. In a Vue on Rails project with Webpacker, how do I use embedded Ruby (Erb) inside your Webpacker project?

Sometimes, you want to use erb inside your Vue component. To do so, please install the erb dependencies into your Webpacker setup:

```
rails webpacker:install:erb
```

4. How do I fix the error "Cannot find module <name_of_module>"?

This error is telling you that Webpack cannot find the <name_of_module> module. Hence, we need to add it via yarn. Run the following command to fix it:

```
yarn add <name_of_module>
```

5. How do I solve an error that says "TypeError: undefined is not an object (evaluating 'options.components')"?

This error is telling you that Webpack cannot find the <name_of_module> module. Hence, we need to add it via yarn. Run the following command to fix it:

```
yarn add <name_of_module>
```

6. In a Vue on Rails project with Webpacker, how do I disable fingerprinting to create Vue.js widget component?

This answer is written by Ross Kaffenberger, an active contributor of Webpacker project on the Webpacker project. The following Webpack plugin helps to produce non-digest assets that do not contain fingerprinting. (https://github.com/rails/webpacker/issues/1310#issuecomment-369721304)

```
// Custom Webpack plugin
// Emits assets with hashed filenames as non-digest filenames
as well
//
// Adding to end of plugins list ensures that all previously
emitted hashed
// assets will be registered prior to executing the
NonDigestAssetsPlugin.

function NonDigestAssetsPlugin() {}

const CHUNKHASH_REGEX = /(-[a-z0-9]{20}\.{1}){1}/;
```

```
NonDigestAssetsPlugin.prototype.apply = function(compiler) {
  compiler.plugin('emit', function(compilation, callback) {
    // Explore each compiled asset in build output:
```

```
Object.entries(compilation.assets).forEach(function([filename,
asset]) {
      if (!CHUNKHASH_REGEX.test(filename)) return;

      // only for filenames matching CHUNKHASH_REGEX
      const nonDigestFilename = filename.replace(CHUNKHASH_
      REGEX, '.');
      compilation.assets[nonDigestFilename] = asset;
  });

  callback();
 });
};
```

```
module.exports = NonDigestAssetsPlugin;
```

7. How do I solve the following Vue error: "Did you register the component correctly? For recursive components, make sure to provide the name option."

This error is pointing to two questions. First, did you register the component correctly?

```
components: {
      'i-tabs' : Tabs,
      'i-tab-pane': Tabpane
  }
```

Second, did you provide the name option in your recursive component?

```
name: 'Tabpane'
```

8. Is there a way to use npm instead of yarn as the default package manager?

For new Rails projects, we can add a flag to the command to bypass yarn and use npm.

```
rails new npm_app --webpack --skip-yarn
```

Now you can install npm packages using the `npm install` command.

9. For Vue on Rails project with Webpacker, how do I manage Node and Rails environments?

Rails uses RAILS_ENV and Node traditionally uses NODE_ENV environment variables to manage whether an app is in development or production. A pull request was merged to ensure these two variables are reconciled.

See **https://github.com/rails/webpacker/pull/1511**

10. For Vue on Rails projects with Webpacker, is there a way to bypass the IE 11 issues on Windows?

IE 11 issues may be caused the UgligyJs plugin not using a downgraded version of ECMA. Try configuring with the following code.

```
const environment = require('./environment')
```

```
environment.plugins.get("UglifyJs").options.uglifyOptions.ecma
= 5
module.exports = environment.toWebpackConfig()
module.exports = NonDigestAssetsPlugin;
```

11. For Vue on Rails projects with Webpacker, shouldn't package X be in the dependencies instead of devDependencies?

The answer lies in how Webpacker works. Webpacker produces JavaScript code called packs that can be embedded into Rails view via the javascript_pack_tag. This requires certain development dependencies to be in the dependencies of package.json.

For further discussion or research, please visit the following links:

```
https://github.com/rails/webpacker/issues/1212
https://github.com/rails/webpacker/issues/1178
```

12. How do I solve this Heroku error: "No default language could be detected for this app"?

If you see the following error message from Heroku console, you need to install the relevant buildpack.

```
remote: Compressing source files... done.
remote: Building source:
remote:
remote: !     No default language could be detected for this
app.
remote:               HINT: This occurs when Heroku cannot detect
the buildpack to use for this application automatically.
```

```
remote:              See https://devcenter.heroku.com/articles/
buildpacks
remote:
remote:  !    Push failed
remote: Verifying deploy...
remote:
remote: !      Push rejected to page-specific-vue-turbolinks.
remote:
To https://git.heroku.com/page-specific-vue-turbolinks.git
 ! [remote rejected]   master -> master (pre-receive hook
declined)
error: failed to push some refs to 'https://git.heroku.com/
page-specific-vue-turbolinks.git'
```

Run the following commands to properly configure the buildpacks for the project.

```
heroku buildpacks:clear
heroku buildpacks:set heroku/nodejs
heroku buildpacks:add heroku/ruby
```

See https://github.com/rails/webpacker/issues/739#
issuecomment-327546884

13. How do I solve this Heroku error: "App not compatible with buildpack"?

When deploying to Heroku, you may see the following error in the output. This means that a package.json file was not found in the app.

```
Counting objects: 16871, done.
Delta compression using up to 4 threads.
Compressing objects: 100% (13035/13035), done.
```

Writing objects: 100% (16871/16871), 17.27 MiB | 1.19 MiB/s,
done.
Total 16871 (delta 2944), reused 16834 (delta 2933)
remote: Compressing source files... done.
remote: Building source:
remote:

**remote: -----> App not compatible with buildpack: https://
buildpack-registry.s3.amazonaws.com/buildpacks/heroku/nodejs.
tgz**
remote: Node.js: package.json not found in application
root
remote:
remote: More info: https://devcenter.heroku.com/
articles/buildpacks#detection-failure
remote:
remote: !   Push failed
remote: Verifying deploy...
remote:
remote: !   Push rejected to page-specific-vue-turbolinks.
remote:
To https://git.heroku.com/page-specific-vue-turbolinks.git
 ! [remote rejected]   master -> master (pre-receive hook
declined)
error: failed to push some refs to 'https://git.heroku.com/
page-specific-vue-turbolinks.git'

To solve this problem, make sure that Webpacker is installed and
a package.json file exists and also that the necessary buildpacks are
installed on Heroku using the following commands.

```
rails webpacker:install
heroku buildpacks:add heroku/nodejs
heroku buildpacks:add heroku/ruby
```

Wrap-up and the Final Step

This concludes the testing, deployment, and troubleshooting chapter of our book. We've shown you how to go from the development phase to a well-tested and deployed production quality application using various testing tools and continuous integration methods. We move on to the final chapter to conclude our book and leave you with some words of wisdom.

CHAPTER 8

Conclusion – Finishing the Race

We hope that you had the light switch moment while reading this book. Web programming is complex but it does not need to be complicated or convoluted. The pursuit of developer happiness and maintainability productivity is endless. But the pursuit can be painless too.

Vue on Rails is not a swiss army knife for all solution. It is a start to an endless pursue to apply a simple approach to web development. This is accomplished through standing firm on two open source giants Rails and Vue.

The race has only just begun. The work of web programmers is endless as the web standard continues to evolve. Vue on Rails represents a movement that promotes cross pollination of developer-friendly frameworks that can only happen because we are standing on the shoulder of open source web giants.

We realize that technologies change at a fast pace and a solution that works today may not be ideal in the future. Even though we believe a Vue on Rails approach is a great combination, a lot of the concepts we discuss hope to open developers' eyes to similar approaches with different technologies such as other MVC frameworks like Django, Java Spring, or .NET Core. I think the best advice is to constantly question an approach

© Bryan Lim and Richard LaFranchi 2019
B. Lim and R. LaFranchi, *Vue on Rails*, https://doi.org/10.1007/978-1-4842-5116-4_8

taken to solve a problem. If you keep doing things the same way, it might get the job done, but then you will never learn a potentially better way that will make your life easier.

Vue is Not Without Guilt

In the past year, Vue 2 has performed very well, in terms of adoption, and comes very close to a corporate-funded React JavaScript framework. In this regard, we feel that Vue has won the race by using an MIT License and is supported by the community rather than influenced largely by a single corporation.

But Vue 2 is not without guilt. For instance, compared to Rails' latest JavaScript approach, Stimulus, Vue 2 is slow and more opinionated in how a developer should approach the frontend. Learning from history, any framework that deviates from the web standard will also not stand the test of a thousand developers' pokes.

Stimulus is also closer to Vanilla JavaScript than Vue itself. Version 1.1 of Stimulus ships with a tiny minified build size of 30kb and carry no extra batteries like state management. Stimulus is twice as fast in rendering speed than Vue and loads less overhead than Vue.js.

With the early review of Vue 3, we see that the performance is fixed and comes with additional benefits like a more modular Vue.js. This means that you can enjoy a smaller Vue.js if you do not use certain aspect of Vue. For instance, if you do not use the transition classes of Vue.js, you can exclude it when you download Vue 3. Vue 3 is faster, smaller, and better in many ways.

Vue 3   Read more about Evan You's plan for Version 3 of Vue.js at `https://tinyurl.com/VuePoint` and his presentation on Vue 3: `https://tinyurl.com/Vue3Pres`.

Ruby on Rails Isn't the Top in Class Either

Ruby on Rails may suffer from performance inadequacy when compared to other web frameworks due to its Ruby language. Ruby language isn't the fastest in the league and that's fine. This is also why the 3 x 3 effort to speed up Ruby the programming language by the Ruby core team is a godsend.

Another famous effort is the ruby-like language Crystal that may have an impact on Rails in the future. Imagine switching out Ruby and having a plugin to reconcile any difference in syntax to enjoy the high-speed railway of concurrency.

Rails and its favorite programming language Ruby 3   Read more on how Ruby has been fast enough at `https://tinyurl.com/RubyFast` and Ruby 3x3 at `https://blog.heroku.com/ruby-3-by-3/`.

Where Do You Go from Here?

Regardless of technology changes in the future, we hope to offer some advice that will stand the test of time:

- If you find yourself performing a lot of repetitive tasks, take some time to automate those tasks using the best tools available.

- Choose simplicity over complexity and convention over configuration.

- Focus on building a great product for your customers.

Don't forget to stay in touch! Here are some ways to stay up to date in the Vue on Rails world:

- Read Vue news `https://news.vuejs.org/`

- Read Ruby on Rails news `https://weblog.rubyonrails.org/news/`

- Become a watcher on the `vueonrails` gem to keep up to date on improvements `https://github.com/vueonrails/vueonrails`

- Follow @ytbryan and @rlafranchi on GitHub

APPENDIX A

The MIT License (MIT) for vuejs.org Content Used in This Book

Copyright (c) 2013-present Yuxi Evan You

Permission is hereby granted, free of charge, to any person obtaining a copy of this software and associated documentation files (the "Software"), to deal in the Software without restriction, including without limitation the rights to use, copy, modify, merge, publish, distribute, sublicense, and/or sell copies of the Software, and to permit persons to whom the Software is furnished to do so, subject to the following conditions:

The above copyright notice and this permission notice shall be included in all copies or substantial portions of the Software.

THE SOFTWARE IS PROVIDED "AS IS", WITHOUT WARRANTY OF ANY KIND, EXPRESS OR IMPLIED, INCLUDING BUT NOT LIMITED TO THE WARRANTIES OF MERCHANTABILITY, FITNESS FOR A PARTICULAR PURPOSE AND NONINFRINGEMENT. IN NO EVENT SHALL THE AUTHORS OR COPYRIGHT HOLDERS BE LIABLE FOR ANY CLAIM, DAMAGES OR OTHER LIABILITY, WHETHER IN AN ACTION OF CONTRACT, TORT OR OTHERWISE, ARISING FROM, OUT OF OR IN CONNECTION WITH THE SOFTWARE OR THE USE OR OTHER DEALINGS IN THE SOFTWARE.

© Bryan Lim and Richard LaFranchi 2019
B. Lim and R. LaFranchi, *Vue on Rails*, https://doi.org/10.1007/978-1-4842-5116-4

Index

A

Action cable
    frontend, 77
    Rails backend, 78
    Vue prototype, 77
    web-socket, 77
activestorage npm package,
    137, 139
Application template
    administrate, 95
    automatic customization, 94
    bootstrap, 96
    development process, 94
    devise, 97
    font awesome icon, 96
    foundation, 96
    Livereload, 97
    rails project, creation, 94
    Sidekiq, 96, 97
    webpacker, 94
    Whenever scheduler, 95
Arrow function, 62
Asset management, 22–24
Asset pipeline, 22–24
Atom editor, 13
Avatar, 136
Axios, 63

B

Behavior-driven development
    (BDD), 157
BrowserStack, 170–173

C

Cheatsheets, 9, 10
Class/style binding
    toggling class, 50
    vue-on-rails.js library, 51
@click event handler, 48
click() method, 49
Computed properties, 48–49
Continuous integration services,
    167–168
croppedGeometry() property, 149
Cropper component, 139–144
Custom test, 168

D

Devise, authentication system, 97

E

el property, 44, 45

F

fileAdded() function, 144
Foundation, 96
Fragile tests, 157

G

GameChannel, 118, 119
Game time, 123, 124
getGame() function, 130
Global event bus, 59

H

Heroku *vs.* virtual private server,
    166, 167
Hybrid app, 20

I

Image-cropping tool
    avatar, 136
    JavaScript libraries, 136
    loading image, 144, 146
    panning the image, 146, 147
    prototype approaches, 135
    scaling, 147–149
    user profile, 137–139
ImageMagick processing, 149, 150
Image scaling, 147–149
Internationalization library,
    105–107
isView() function, 87

J

join(piece) method, 125

K

Keeping programmer insanely
    (KPI), 17, 18

L

Lifecycle hook, 44, 132
Listing games, 121, 122
Livereload, 97

M

MIT License (MIT), 187
Mixins, 52, 53
Modern web application, 19
    attributes, 20
    cross-platform development, 19
    goodness test, 22
    hybrid app, 20
    Ruby on Rails, 22
    use, 20, 21
Monolithic rails architecture, 85, 86
mounted() lifecycle, 144

N, O

Nested form, Vue component,
    90–94
newGame() method, 122
Ninja deployment, 165

P, Q

pan() method, 147
Panning the image, 146–147
Properties *vs.* data, 45, 46

R

Rails first approach
    functionality, 29
    version 1, 27–29
Rails-first Vue first-class
        approach, 41–42
Reactivity system, 39
Resources, 10, 11
Router
    file creation, 65, 66
    initialization, 66, 67
    parameter, 68, 69
    redirect/alert, 69, 71
    <router-link>, 67, 68
    SPA, 71
    vue-router npm package, 64
Routing parameter, 68–69
Ruby on Rails doctrine, 13

S

Search engine optimized (SEO), 100
Server-side rendering (SSR), 100
    i18n Vue, 107–110
    internationalization library,
        105–107
    manual configuration, 101,
        103–105

scaffolders, 101, 102
SEO friendly, 100
web pages, 100
Sidekiq, 96–97
Simple polling, 78–79
Simple state management
    GitHub, 111, 112
    scaffolders, 112, 113
    timestamp, 110
    Vuex, 110
Single-page application (SPA), 3,
    17, 84
Single source of truth (SSOT), 72
Specific-page Vue (SPV)
    application template, 86
    components, 84
    monolithic rails architecture, 85
    pages/index.html view, 86
    pages/second.html view, 87
    SPA approach, 85
    Turbolinks, 89, 90
    web app lifecycle, 85
SSR, *see* Server-side rendering (SSR)
Sublime text, 13
System tests, 158–160

T

Test-driven development
    (TDD), 156
Testing approaches
    general guidelines, 157
    low-consequence project, 156
    regression tests, 155

Testing approaches (*cont.*)
RSpec and BDD, 157
software testing, 155
system tests, 158–160
TDD, 156
test utilities and jest, 160
Vue unit test, 161
Tic Tac Toe board component,
162–165
toggleClass() method, 51
Tool versions, 9, 10
Tradeoffs, 16
Travis CI, 168, 169
Troubleshooting, 173–181
Two-player game
action cable
chat app, 115
consumer, 131, 132
software design, 116
Vuex rails plugin, 132
websockets, 115
controllers, 119, 120
creation, 122, 123
domain model, 117, 118
game channel, 118, 119
listing games, 121, 122
Tic Tac Toe game, 116, 125–130

U

UI compatibility, Vue, 97–99
User profile, 137–139

V

Virtual DOM, 29
Virtual private servers
(VPS), 166
Visual Studio Code, 11
tools, 12
Vue
components (*see* Vue
components)
data
characteristics, 46
v-model directive, 47
data variable, 4
directives, 47
JavaScript environment, 5
lifecycle, 42, 43
manual enabling, 99, 100
objectives, 7, 8
pass data, server, 60, 62
HTTP client, 62
peer-to-peer protocol, 4
plugins, 51
on Rails, 5, 6
router (*see* Router)
web application, 6
Vue components
flash notices/alerts, 56–59
global registration, 60
local registration, 60
Vue on Rails project, 53, 54
x-template, 54–56

Vue Devtool, 93
Vue first approach
    advantages, 33
    application, 30
    disadvantages, 33
    single-page application, 34
    version 2, 30–32
Vue first *vs.* Rails first
    KPI, 17, 18
    requirement, 15
    SPA, 17
    tradeoffs, 16
    web application, 15
Vue-first/Rails-only approach
    advantages, 37, 38
    disadvantages, 38
    MVC pattern, 35
    reactivity, 39
    reusability, 38, 39
    version 3, 36, 37
    webpacker, 35

Vue on Rails, 6, 183
    MIT license, 184
    MVC frameworks, 183
    projects, 25–27
vue-resource, 63
Vuex
    installation, 73
    manage states, 72, 73
    rails plugin
        configuration, 74
        posts#index action, 75, 76
    state management tools, 72

W, X, Y, Z

Watch method, 48, 49
Webpack, 23
Webpacker, 23
    approach, 24
    asset pipeline, 24
    installation, 25

Printed in the United States
By Bookmasters